Acting Edition

Exit Who?
A Farce in Two Acts

by Fred Carmichael

Copyright © 1982 by Fred Carmichael
All Rights Reserved

EXIT WHO? is fully protected under the copyright laws of the United States of America, the British Commonwealth, including Canada, and all member countries of the Berne Convention for the Protection of Literary and Artistic Works, the Universal Copyright Convention, and/or the World Trade Organization conforming to the Agreement on Trade Related Aspects of Intellectual Property Rights. All rights, including professional and amateur stage productions, recitation, lecturing, public reading, motion picture, radio broadcasting, television, online/digital production, and the rights of translation into foreign languages are strictly reserved.

ISBN 9780573618772

www.concordtheatricals.com
www.concordtheatricals.co.uk

FOR PRODUCTION INQUIRIES

UNITED STATES AND CANADA
info@concordtheatricals.com
1-866-979-0447

UNITED KINGDOM AND EUROPE
licensing@concordtheatricals.co.uk
020-7054-7298

Each title is subject to availability from Concord Theatricals Corp., depending upon country of performance. Please be aware that *EXIT WHO?* may not be licensed by Concord Theatricals Corp. in your territory. Professional and amateur producers should contact the nearest Concord Theatricals Corp. office or licensing partner to verify availability.

CAUTION: Professional and amateur producers are hereby warned that *EXIT WHO?* is subject to a licensing fee. The purchase, renting, lending or use of this book does not constitute a license to perform this title(s), which license must be obtained from Concord Theatricals Corp. prior to any performance. Performance of this title(s) without a license is a violation of federal law and may subject the producer and/or presenter of such performances to civil penalties. Both amateurs and professionals considering a production are strongly advised to apply to the appropriate agent before starting rehearsals, advertising, or booking a theatre. A licensing fee must be paid whether the title(s) is presented for charity or gain and whether or not admission is charged. Professional/Stock licensing fees are quoted upon application to Concord Theatricals Corp.

This work is published by Samuel French, an imprint of Concord Theatricals Corp.

No one shall make any changes in this title(s) for the purpose of production. No part of this book may be reproduced, stored in a retrieval system, scanned, uploaded, or transmitted in any form, by any means, now known or yet to be invented, including mechanical, electronic, digital, photocopying, recording, videotaping, or otherwise, without the prior written permission of the publisher. No one shall share this title(s), or any part of this title(s), through any social media or file hosting websites.

For all inquiries regarding motion picture, television, online/digital and other media rights, please contact Concord Theatricals Corp.

MUSIC AND THIRD-PARTY MATERIALS USE NOTE

Licensees are solely responsible for obtaining formal written permission from copyright owners to use copyrighted music and/or other copyrighted third-party materials (e.g., artworks, logos) in the performance of this play and are strongly cautioned to do so. If no such permission is obtained by the licensee, then the licensee must use only original music and materials that the licensee owns and controls. Licensees are solely responsible and liable for clearances of all third-party copyrighted materials, including without limitation music, and shall indemnify the copyright owners of the play(s) and their licensing agent, Concord Theatricals Corp., against any costs, expenses, losses and liabilities arising from the use of such copyrighted third-party materials by licensees. For music, please contact the appropriate music licensing authority in your territory for the rights to any incidental music.

IMPORTANT BILLING AND CREDIT REQUIREMENTS

If you have obtained performance rights to this title, please refer to your licensing agreement for important billing and credit requirements.

CAST

(in order of appearance)

WILFRED WOOSTER
CRANE HAMMOND
JOEL DOVER
KATE BIXLEY
VERNON COOKLEY
JEWEL
LYDIA SCOTT
CYRUS D. CONWAY
MABEL

SCENE

The living room of a house in Vermont.

TIME

ACT ONE – A July afternoon. The present.

ACT TWO –
    SCENE 1: Evening. The same day.
    SCENE 2: Later that same evening.

Exit Who?

ACT ONE

SCENE: *The entire action of the play takes place in the living room of a New England house which has been rented for the month of August. The room is tastefully decorated and furnished showing the hand of an experienced decorator. Down R. is a straight-backed chair, immediately above it French windows leading off R.. In the up R. corner is a what-not shelf with objets d'art. Up R. on the back wall and towards C. is a closet, the door of which opens into the room and is hinged on the R. The interior is painted a lighter shade than the room to make it more focal. On the inside R. wall of the closet is another door which opens off to the library. It is necessary that the audience have a complete view of the closet when it is opened. Immediately to the L. of the closet a short wall goes Upstage forming the outside wall of the closet and also the wall of the hallway. Between the Upstage part of this and the Upstage wall of the house is a passageway which also leads Off R. to the library. Directly Up C. on the back wall is a door opening Onstage and to the R. This leads to the outside and the path from the house runs Off L. To the L. of the door is a stairway leading upstairs. The entire hallway is framed by an archway from the living room. On the Up L. wall, there is a built-in bookcase, the bottom shelf is wider than the rest and is used for a bar. Downstage on the L. wall is a swinging door which leads to the kitchen. The furniture consists of a two-seater sofa, right near the French windows with a small table to the R. of it, a small stuffed armchair C. with a small table to its R., and a desk, flat-topped is stage L. in front of the bookcase-bar with a small desk chair to the L. of it facing the room. The desk is almost perpendicular to the audience and has the telephone Upstage and a desk lamp. Since this is a farce, the colors are bright and harmonious and the sun is streaming in through the French windows. At the moment, the chair C. and the sofa are covered with dust sheets as the house is unoccupied.*

AT RISE: COLONEL WILFRED WOOSTER *comes to the French windows and opens them. He is an elderly, retired colonel who is always trying to please everyone but is very vague and confused due to approaching senility. He is always happy and charging ahead with his present ideas. He carries a bunch of small flowers he has just picked. He goes to the what-not shelf Up R. and takes down a vase, notices the furniture is covered, clucks about it and exits into the kitchen through the swinging door. As door closes, the front door opens and* CRANE HAMMOND *is standing there with two suitcases. She looks at the covered furniture disapprovingly.*

CRANE. Well, really. (*Goes upstairs.* WILFRED *enters immediately with his flowers, puts them on the desk, picks up a pile of books there and starts for the library, notices the covered furniture again and mutters.*)

WILFRED. Well, really. (*Exits library.* CRANE *comes downstairs immediately and goes out the front door.* CRANE *is an attractive woman in her late thirties or early forties. She has a warm smile and a delightful personality and enjoys life to the fullest.* WILFRED *comes in from the library immediately and goes upstairs.* CRANE *returns with her purse and some long-stemmed flowers wrapped in florist's paper. She puts them on the desk, goes to the closet and hangs up her light topcoat, returns to the desk, looks at the short-stemmed flowers in the vase, takes paper off her flowers, removes the short-stemmed ones and puts hers in the vase, and takes the old flowers and the florist paper and goes into the kitchen.* WILFRED *comes downstairs, sees the flowers in the vase and mutters.*) Amazing. (*Starts for kitchen as* CRANE *comes in the swinging door and they are face to face.* CRANE *gives a startled gasp.*)

CRANE. You startled me.
WILFRED. Sorry, I didn't know you were here.
CRANE. What can I do for you?
WILFRED. (*Moves away* R.) The first thing would be to remove the dust covers.
CRANE. I certainly intend to.
WILFRED. Don't know why you put them on.
CRANE. I didn't. I—
WILFRED. Do you do windows? On a clear day you can see New Hampshire.
CRANE. Who do you think I am, the cleaning lady?
WILFRED. Aren't you?
CRANE. I think we'd better start all over. (*Moves to him and extends her hand.*) How do you do? I'm Crane Hammond.
WILFRED. (*Shakes hands, then look at her confused.*) Of course, so sorry. Forgot I'd invited you.
CRANE. You didn't invite me. I—
WILFRED. Well, who did?
CRANE. No one. I—

WILFRED. Oh, you're looking for a room. Bed and breakfast and that sort of thing. I don't know how much to charge.

CRANE. (*Giving up.*) Do you mind telling me your name?

WILFRED. Don't you know me?

CRANE. No.

WILFRED. Pity. I know myself, of course. I'm—er—

CRANE. Yes.

WILFRED. I'll have it in a minute. Right on the tip of my tongue. Age, you know. Forget names. It'll come to me. (*Stares into space and mutters some names to himself.*)

CRANE. Perhaps you have some identification on you. American Express, driver's license. I'll even accept Master Charge.

WILFRED. Got it! Told you it was right here. (*Points to the tip of his tongue.*) Feel better now.

CRANE. Well, what is it?

WILFRED. What?

CRANE. Your name.

WILFRED. Wooster. Wilfred Wooster. Lt. Colonel Wooster at your service.

CRANE. Retired?

WILFRED. Certainly. Uniform in moth balls. Now, what can I do for you?

CRANE. You can tell me what you're doing here.

WILFRED. I live here.

CRANE. I think you're confused. I live here. I have rented this place starting today. I have rented it once before. I may rent it again.

WILFRED. Are you sure?

CRANE. I have a lease.

WILFRED. (*Crosses below sofa and Up R. looking at room.*) Looks like my house. No souvenirs though. No photos of the troops. Not a single medal on display.

CRANE. (*Moves in below chair* C.) Perhaps I should call a doctor.

WILFRED. That's not necessary, my dear. I know how to find out. (*Goes to phone on Upstage end of desk.*)

CRANE. Is there a missing persons bureau in the village?

WILFRED. (*Into phone.*) Mabel, this is . . . (*To* CRANE.) What did I say my name was?

CRANE. Lt. Colonel Wooster.

WILFRED. Thank you, you're being very helpful.

CRANE. (*Leans back on chair arm.*) I aim to please.

WILFRED. (*Into phone.*) I am Lt. Colonel Wooster . . . Mabel, dear, would you do me a favor and tell me where I am calling from? . . . Oh, really. Dear, dear . . . (*To* CRANE.) Wrong house. (*Back to phone.*) This looks like my house, doesn't it, Mabel? . . . You're right. I forgot about the flaming celosia out front. Thank you, dear, and say hello to . . . whatever-his-name-is-your-husband. (*Hangs up.*) I'm frightfully embarrassed.

CRANE. Where *do* you live?

WILFRED. Down the road two houses.

CRANE. (*Goes to him.*) Of course. I've seen your flaming celosia in the front yard.

WILFRED. Beautiful plant. You can dry it, you know, if you have the time.

CRANE. (*Puts her arm through his and guides him to the front door.*) Not today, Colonel. I have to unpack. Perhaps we can have a drink together some time.

WILFRED. Sounds delightful.

CRANE. Last time I rented this house I worked the whole time and never got to socialize.

WILFRED. (*Starts to put* CRANE *out the door.*) You'll call then?

CRANE. Just as soon as I'm settled in.

WILFRED. Thanks so much for stopping by and we'll have that drink together real soon. (*Starts to close the door with* CRANE *outside.*)

CRANE. (*Pushes door back open and comes in.*) No, no. I live here. You live with the flaming celosia.

WILFRED. (*Steps outside.*) Of course. Of course. Sorry about that. I'll remember next time.

CRANE. (*Indicates Off* L.) You're right down there.

WILFRED. I know, my dear. I've lived there for — er — ever so many years.

CRANE. It was very nice to meet you.

WILFRED. Yes, wasn't it? And it was nice to meet you. Good day, Mrs. Wooster. (*Ambles off.* CRANE *closes the door and goes to the phone.*)

CRANE. (*Looks for dial and doesn't see one.*) Unbelievable. (*Into phone.*) Mabel, this is . . . yes, it is . . . thank you. I've rented it again for a month . . . of course you would know already. (*Sits in the desk chair.*) Mabel, I can't believe you're still there. I thought all operators had been replaced by dials . . . the last holdout in the country? . . . I'd sign any petition that will keep your job. Tell me, Mabel, a Lt. Colonel Wooster just . . . yes, delightful, but a little odd, don't you think? . . . It's better than a nursing home, I agree, but should he be out alone? . . . If everyone does pitch together, of course you can see he keeps getting home. (*Rises.*) Thanks, Mabel. I'll check on him. I don't think he'll disturb me again. I hope not. I have lots of work to do. (*Hangs up.*) That's it. No more disturbances. (*Takes sheet off chair* C. *and rolls it under her arm.*) From now on, work, work, work. (*Goes to* C. *end of sofa and takes hold of the sheet.*) No looking at the scenery. (*Focuses on the view from the windows.*) Just once. One long look. (*Holding onto sheet, she walks below the sofa to the windows. As she pulls the sheet off behind her, we see* JOEL DOVER *lying there, his eyes staring at the retreating* CRANE. *A man of about thirty, he is dressed in slacks and open-necked shirt with a sports jacket.*) Not a soul in sight. (*She backs up perching on the* R. *sofa arm.* JOEL *rises quietly and backs away from her, looks frantically for somewhere to hide, decides on the closet. As he closes the door,* CRANE *crosses below the sofa with the sheets, takes her purse from the desk and goes upstairs.*) It certainly is peaceful. (JOEL *opens closet door slightly and peeks out. The front door opens, he ducks back in the closet as* KATE BIXLEY *stands in the front door.* KATE *is about* CRANE'S *age, an efficient secretary and more than that, a friend. Her slightly jaundiced look at life is not too heartfelt and she enjoys herself greatly.*)

KATE. (*Stands there looking at the room. She has a topcoat on and is holding a suitcase and a portable typewriter. Puts the luggage down. To herself.*) What am I doing here? I'm not a country girl. I belong in a high-rise on Central Park South, not a no-rise in Vermont. Oh, well. (*Calls.*) Crane.

CRANE. (*Off Stage.*) Kate, is that you?

KATE. If this is Sunnybrook Farm, Rebecca has arrived.

CRANE. (*Off Stage.*) I can't wait to see you.

KATE. I've aged. It's the air. I'm wrinkling like a prune.

CRANE. (*Runs downstairs.*) Kate. (*Throws arms around her.*)

KATE. (*Smiles.*) Hello, Crane.

CRANE. I was afraid you wouldn't show up.

KATE. Sorry I'm late. I had to go back for my passport. I could have sworn there was a border to cross between New York and Vermont.

CRANE. The same old Kate. Sit down. Tell me

everything about your vacation. Here, let me take your coat. (*Takes her coat and goes to closet.*)

KATE. (*Crosses to windows.*) It was absolutely fabulous. I did Europe the way I wanted to. I'd sit in a little cafe in Paris and watch all those American Express people get herded into buses and rushed out to Versailles.

CRANE. (*Opens closet. It is empty. Hangs* KATE'S *coat up.*) Versailles is beautiful.

KATE. (*Sits sofa* R.) I know. I bought three postcards of it on the Champs Elysée.

CRANE. The gardens are spectacular.

KATE. Can't beat my philodendron on West 73rd Street.

CRANE. (*Sits by* KATE.) And Rome? Did you go down to Capri? The Blue Grotto and all that?

KATE. I didn't stray very far from the Via Veneto. The shops are fantastic.

CRANE. And the Trevi Fountain? You did throw in a coin, didn't you?

KATE. I made my wish and it worked. I tossed my coin, it hit the edge and bounced right out again.

CRANE. So you didn't stray from the cities at all?

KATE. I did museums everywhere, Crane. Museums and churches and shops. I did what I wanted to.

CRANE. But the country—

KATE. When I was four years old, my mother took me to Central Park and I saw a tree. Once you've seen one, you've seen them all.

CRANE. You just don't like nature.

KATE. I don't like being out-numbered. (*Rises and goes to French windows.*) Look out there. Acres and acres of trees. If they ever get a leader, we're finished.

CRANE. To each his own. As long as you enjoyed yourself.

KATE. (*Goes above the sofa.*) I'll give you your present later.

CRANE. Oh, you didn't have to.

KATE. (*Moves* C.) Of course I had to. When an employer gives her Girl Friday a three week vacation with pay, she has to bring her back something worth at least five thousand lira. (*Sits on arm of chair* C.) Let's see, at the current exchange rate, that comes to—

CRANE. I don't need a present. I want one but I don't need one. I have everything I want.

KATE. You won the lottery?

CRANE. I have the next book. Right up here. (*Taps forehead.*)

KATE. In that desert of a mind, you found an oasis?

CRANE. (*Goes to windows.*) It came to me suddenly one day while I was in the A&P.

KATE. I didn't know Bronxville had an A&P. I thought it was Neiman-Marcus or nothing.

CRANE. You would have been proud of me. I was using my cents-off coupons. I saw a woman shoplift a persimmon.

KATE. (*Moves to sofa and sits.*) Why, in God's name would anyone shoplift at the A&P? Be reckless. Try Tiffany's.

CRANE. Anyway, the manager saw her and chased her from the vegetable counter down past the Bold and Downy. She careened past the Bounce, doubled-back at the Fresh Start and headed up by the Goya Beans. He cut her off right where Aunt Millie's sauce meets Uncle Ben's rice.

KATE. You've decided to write a cook book?

CRANE. No. The chase. (*Crosses up* C.) It started my mind going again on international intrigue, and by the time I'd diven home I had the whole plot of the next book.

KATE. And that's how best-sellers are born.

CRANE. That's how. (*Goes to* KATE, S.L.) It's been two years, Kate. Two long, dry, arrid, idealess years.

KATE. During which I have copied two magazine articles for you, answered your fan mail, made TV talk show appointments, and cheated on your income tax. But I have missed those long hours at my IBM Selectric.

CRANE. (*Sits in chair* C.) This is going to be the best yet. Don't forget, three out of five of my books made the Times Top Ten.

KATE. Two out of Five.

CRANE. But I've never been at the very top. I've made sixth place and the last book made fourth.

KATE. Fifth.

CRANE. Who quibbles over one point?

KATE. The New York Stock Exchange for one, the National Football League—

CRANE. All right. I made sixth and fifth, but this is going to be number one.

KATE. You amaze me, Crane, you really do. To look at you, who would ever think you were not only a successful writer but a good one. The two don't always go together.

CRANE. Why, thank you, Kate.

KATE. You're the best suspense novelist since Agatha Christie.

CRANE. No, that's Helen McInnes. I'm number two but I am trying harder.

KATE. What about that husband of yours? I read in the Herald International he's signed for another book.

CRANE. Richard is in Los Angeles right now talking about a screen treatment of his first one.

KATE. How can they make a movie of it? It's so deep. I loved it, of course. It was beautiful and challenging and encouraging. I just didn't understand it.

CRANE. He deserves every bit of his success. How many years did he write that miserable Lonleyhearts column? Five?

KATE. Four. He was Dorothy Duckworth for four years.

CRANE. He didn't like being a woman at all. Says he can't understand why I'm one, but he's glad I am.

KATE. That's good. I don't think he and Gore Vidal would hit it off.

CRANE. (*Rises and goes to her.*) Come on, Kate. We can't sit here all day. Don't you want to unpack?

KATE. (*Rises.*) All I need is three hangers and a washcloth. When I came in from the airport and saw your note, I left one bag and brought the other. Everything's wash and dry.

CRANE. (*Moves below the sofa as she cases the room.*) Can you believe it, Kate? This place hasn't changed an iota.

KATE. The good die young.

CRANE. The same furniture, the same carpet, the same paint.

KATE. (*Goes to bar.*) The same bar.

CRANE. (*Goes Up R.*) And well-stocked, too. There aren't many places you can rent where everything is ready for you right down to salt in the shakers.

KATE. But don't you get odd feelings when you remember what happened here last time?

CRANE. That was nothing.

KATE. (*Goes Up C.*) I don't call crooks, missing jewels, and bodies hanging in that closet nothing.

CRANE. (*Goes to her.*) It all worked out for the best. We found the missing diamonds, didn't we? And none of the bodies was dead and we went on to write a good story.

KATE. I've been suspicious of showers ever since I saw

PSYCHO and downright intimidated by closets ever since you first opened that one.

CRANE. Don't be silly. We had a marvelous month and that's why I came back here to do the first draft of the new book.

KATE. Promise you won't get involved in anything like last time?

CRANE. (*Goes to closet.*) If the house didn't have this peculiar closet that goes through to the library I never would have written that story for REDBOOK and you might have been out of a job.

KATE. I love that closet more than I can say.

CRANE. (*Opens it. It is empty.*) Remember when Vernon Cookley was standing in there and I thought—

KATE. (*Goes to her.*) Vernon Cookley. Is he still around with his polished Steriff's badge?

CRANE. He has to be. Verne is part of this place.

KATE. Like the Gypsy Moth and the septic tanks.

CRANE. I wonder if they still have all my books in the library? I left a complete set. (*Walks through closet and opens door in R. wall of the closet and goes Off Stage into the library.*)

KATE. (*Follows her through. As* KATE *goes through,* JOEL *appears from the library into the hall Up* C.. *As he comes out, he circles below the closet after* KATE *is out of sight.*) The winter was so cold they might have been used for kindling.

CRANE. (*Off Stage, laughing.*) Kate!

KATE. (*Off Stage.*) Same rows of books. Everything from the Farmer's Almanac to the National Geographic. August '34. It's a collector's item.

CRANE. (*Off Stage.*) Here we are. All my books are still here.

KATE. (*Off Stage.*) There's dust on them. They haven't been read.

CRANE. (*Comes through into hall Up* C. *just as* JOEL *closes closet door.*) It's the principle of the thing. They weren't stolen by other tenants.

KATE. (*Comes out of library.*) I hope they were as thoughtful of the towels.

CRANE. It's really nice to be back here. You don't really mind it, do you? (*Reaches back to close the closet door and is surprised to find it already shut.*)

KATE. It's all right, I guess. But it's so quiet. (*Sits on the Upstage end of the desk.*) If I could only hear a siren or an occasional cry of "Stop thief!"

CRANE. (*Goes to above* KATE.) You'll have excitement enough once I start dictating. Most of the book takes place in the major cities of Europe. Crowds, traffic jams, milling throngs. You'll love it.

KATE. (*Opens front door.*) Then I'd better get my work bag from the car. Lots of clean paper, a new typewriter ribbon, and —

CRANE. And correction fluid, or have you taken a Katherine Gibbs refresher?

KATE. Very funny. (*Starts off* L.)

CRANE. I'll go and unpack.

KATE. (*Pokes head back in.*) Oh, no, you won't.

CRANE. Why not?

KATE. Here comes Grover's Corners answer to Robert Redford. (*Goes off and we hear her talking.*) Hello, there, Mr. Cookley. Nice to see you again.

VERNON. (*Off Stage.*) Ayah. Same here.

CRANE. Vernon Cookley, is that you?

VERNON. (*Enters. He is a typical Vermonter of indeterminate age. Very little excites* VERNON *as he goes about life. He wears a shirt with no tie, a vest, and an ever-present felt hat.*) If t'ain't, I don't know where I am.

CRANE. It's so nice to see you again.

VERNON. Likewise. (*Tips his hat.*)

CRANE. I bet you're surprised to see us here.

VERNON. Can't say I am. Mabel spilled the beans.

CRANE. She still listens in at the switchboard?

VERNON. Ayah. Says it's better than AS THE WORLD TURNS.

CRANE. Come in. Sit down.

VERNON. Don't mind if I do. (*He sits chair C. and* CRANE *sits on the sofa during the following.*) Can't stay long though. Got my duties.

CRANE. Don't tell me crime has raised its ugly head up here?

VERNON. Gettin' pretty bad. Someone broke the candy machine at the movie house. Took three Baby Ruths and one Butterfinger.

CRANE. That's terrible.

VERNON. Can't eat Baby Ruth myself. Nuts get under my plate.

CRANE. (*After a pause.*) Well, what else is new?

VERNON. Nothin'.

CRANE. (*Another pause.*) How's your wife?

VERNON. Ain't changed.

CRANE. (*Pause.*) It certainly is nice to be back.

VERNON. Wouldn't know how it is to come back. Never been away.

KATE. (*Comes in door with briefcase containing paper, checkbook, pen. Puts it on the desk.*) You having a bright little conversation?

VERNON. Ayah.

KATE. How's your wife?

VERNON. Already been through that with Mrs. Hammond.

KATE. Sorry. (*Takes luggage she first brought in upstairs.*)

CRANE. Is there something special we can do for you, Vernon?

VERNON. Ayah.

CRANE. (*Pause.*) What is it?

VERNON. You're breakin' the law.

CRANE. I'm not parked on the wrong side of the street. I'm in the driveway.

VERNON. T'ain't that.

CRANE. Then what?

VERNON. You're trespassin'.

CRANE. Nonsense. I rented this house for a month. I have the lease. (*As* KATE *comes downstairs.*) Kate, Vernon says we're trespassing.

KATE. (*Goes to desk and sits in chair.*) You have the lease, don't you?

CRANE. Of course.

VERNON. For the month of August.

CRANE. That's right.

VERNON. This is July.

CRANE. No, it's the first of August.

VERNON. T'ain't.

CRANE. Thirty days hath September, April, June, and November. All the rest have thirty-one except Oh, — my — God, it is the thirty-first of July.

KATE. And I gave you my drug store calendar for Christmas.

CRANE. (*Rises and goes to windows,.*) This is terrible.

VERNON. Ayah. It's a crime.

CRANE. No wonder the furniture was still covered.

VERNON. Jewel is supposed to get it ready for you.

CRANE. Jewel?

KATE. Sounds like a gem.

VERNON. (*Rises and goes to desk.*) Ayah. Man who rented this place last ran out before the month was up.

City fella. Didn't trust him as far as I could throw him.

KATE. (*Ever so interested.*) And how far would that be, Mr. Cookley?

VERNON. (*Points.*) Oh, from here to there.

KATE. That's what I like—specifics.

VERNON. (*Goes* C.) He left and Jewel came and covered the furniture. She was goin' to clean tomorrow since Mrs. Scott said you was comin' in the late afternoon of the first.

CRANE. That's right, but—

KATE. Who is Mrs. Scott?

VERNON. Lydia Scott, real estate lady. Took over when Helen O'Toole went to jail. You helped catch her as that jewel thief. Don't you remember?

KATE. Vividly.

CRANE. (*Moves above sofa.*) Then all we have to do is pay an extra day's rent.

VERNON. (*Goes to her.*) What about Jewel? You took the sheets off the furniture?

KATE. Perhaps we could put them on again and then this Jewel could take them off. Would that be all right, Verne?

VERNON. Nope. Jewel is supposed to clean and cook. She's a codocil in your lease.

CRANE. Perhaps she could clean tomorrow.

VERNON. (*Starts for front door.*) You'll have to ask her that.

KATE. I have this sinking feeling Jewel is outside.

VERNON. (*Calling out.*) Jewel, get yourself in here.

KATE. I'll give you five to three she's barefoot.

VERNON. (*Comes back in to below closet.*) Jewel is a good worker. Handy, too. Won first prize at the County Fair last Summer.

CRANE. Quilting?

VERNON. Log-splitting. (JEWEL *enters. She is a very large Vermont farm woman, she takes no guff from anyone. A very definite person, she possesses an extremely low voice. She is wearing a cotton print dress.*)

JEWEL. (*Walks to* KATE *and speaks ominously.*) Who took the dust covers off?

KATE. It wasn't me. (*Holds up hand.*) Scout's honor.

CRANE. (*Comes in below chair* C.) I did it, Jewel. I'm very sorry.

JEWEL. (*Goes to her.*) You Mrs. Hammond?

CRANE. Yes, I am.

JEWEL. I read some of your books.

CRANE. Thank you.

JEWEL. For what?

CRANE. I thought maybe you liked them.

JEWEL. Did. 'Specially them real racy spots. Like A SPY TO DIE. In that hotel room. Page 161.

KATE. I had to turn the lights out when I typed it.

JEWEL. That was somethin'. How do you know about them things?

CRANE. I steal from Masters and Johnson. I'm sorry we got here a day early but I'm sure everything will work out all right.

JEWEL. I gotta cook for you. Lease says so. Except Thursday.

VERNON. And this here's Friday.

KATE. Lucky us.

JEWEL. I checked the larder this mornin'. The refrigerator has three Baby Ruth's and one Butterfinger.

VERNON. That solves that crime.

JEWEL. Ate the Butterfinger but didn't touch the Baby Ruths.

CRANE. Nuts get under your plate?

JEWEL. How'd you know?

KATE. Crane, you's psychic.
CRANE. I tell you what, Jewel . . .
JEWEL. What?
CRANE. You go to the store and get in supplies for dinner. Charge it to me. I'm sure Mr. Perkins will let me reopen my account.
JEWEL. He'll do what I tell him. He's my husband.
CRANE. Will you tell him then?
JEWEL. That I will. I knew I'd like you, Mrs. Hammond, as soon as I read Page 161.
KATE. You'd love reading the IRT subway stop at 63rd.
JEWEL. You a guest here?
KATE. No, I work for Mrs. Hammond. (*Rises and extends her hand.*) I'm Kate Bixley, her secretary.
JEWEL. What's she need you for?
KATE. I take dictation and copy her golden words.
JEWEL. (*To* CRANE.) Why don't you take a typin' course? They advertise them things on the back of matchbooks.
CRANE. Yes, I guess I could.
JEWEL. (*To* KATE.) Why else does she need you?
KATE. Well, I—(*To* CRANE *as she sits at desk again.*) Why else do you need me?
CRANE. (*Goes below sofa and sits.*) Let me count the ways.
VERNON. (*To* JEWEL.) You get the food, Jewel, and cook them up a hearty New England dinner.
KATE. I'm crazy about chocolate mousse.
JEWEL. Ain't never heard of cookin' moose with chocolate.
KATE. That was a joke. You see, mousse is a dessert and Moose is also an animal and . . . (*Looks at* JEWEL's *blank face.*) Oh, I reckon you better skip it.

JEWEL. Ayah.
CRANE. Just something light will be fine, Jewel.
JEWEL. (*Goes to front door.*) I'll be back quicker than you can say apple pan dowdy.
KATE. I won't even try.
JEWEL. (*As* VERNON *starts for front door.*) You don't need to drive me, Verne. I'll cut across Claude's pasture.
VERNON. Watch out for that bull.
JEWEL. He'd better watch out for me. (*Exits.*)
KATE. That one could make a fortune in New York being a mugger. Who could resist her saying. (*Imitates* JEWEL.) "Give me your money!"
VERNON. Jewel's got a heart of gold.
CRANE. She's even built like Fort Knox.
VERNON. Well, I better be gettin' on my horse.
KATE. No wonder Jewel didn't want a ride with you.
VERNON. It's a figure of speech. Oh, I see. You was bein' funny again, Miss Bixley.
KATE. You got it.
CRANE. (*Goes to* VERNON.) Thanks for stopping by, Verne. We'll see that Mrs. Scott is paid an extra day's rent.
VERNON. When Mabel called and told me you was here, I just dropped my coffee cup and rushed right over. (*Tips his hat.*) Nice to have you back, Mrs. Hammond. (*Tips hat again.*) You, too, Miss Bixley. You're a funny one. I'm not sure how to take you.
KATE. Why don't you wait till I offer?
VERNON. Just call if you want anythin'. I'll be seein' you on Thursday anyway.
CRANE. You will?
VERNON. That's the day I pick up the garbage.
CRANE. You do that, too?
VERNON. Gotta make a livin'. (WILFRED *comes*

through the kitchen door carrying his original flowers.)

WILFRED. (*Goes Down* C.) Sorry to interrupt but I forgot my flowers. I seem to have left them in the kitchen garbage. Strange.

CRANE. I'm glad you remembered, Colonel. This is my secretary, Kate Bixley, and, of course, you know this man. (VERNON *comes down to him.*)

WILFRED. Delighted to meet you, Mr. Hammond.

VERNON. Now, Colonel. You know me. Look again.

WILFRED. Vernon Cookley. Of course. You're always picking me up when I'm in the wrong house. I know this isn't mine though. It's Mrs. Hammond's and her charming daughter. (*Looks at* KATE.)

KATE. Could I have that again?

CRANE. She is my secretary.

WILFRED. Yes, that's what I said. (*Goes to front door.*) Well, I have to get home now for — for something or other. I'll think of it when I get there.

VERNON. (*Cross Upstage.*) And Mrs. Hammond has to start writin'. She's a famous author. It takes a lot of work.

WILFRED. I'm sure it does.

KATE. But Crane can do it. She's Herculean.

CRANE. (*Goes to windows.*) I'm Titanic.

WILFRED. (*In doorway.*) Ah, the Titanic. Don't remind me. I was on it, you know?

CRANE. The ship?

WILFRED. Yes. Crash into that iceberg we went. Stood there singing "Nearer My God to Thee".

KATE. What happened to you?

WILFRED. Went down with the ship. A tragedy. A great tragedy. They never found me, you know. (*Exits.*)

KATE. And what, may I ask, was that?

CRANE. Colonel Wilfred Wooster.

KATE. Did he fight on our side?

CRANE. He lives up the road apiece in the house with the flaming celosia.

VERNON. Nice man, the Colonel. A mite vague though. You might have noticed.

KATE. I noticed.

VERNON. Has a housekeeper. She tends to him fine and as long as us villagers see he gets home when he shows up at the wrong house. People always set an extra place at a dinner party 'cause you never know when he'll pop up. You can always count on him at barbeques 'cause he sees the smoke.

CRANE. (*Moves above sofa.*) I bet he doesn't miss a funeral.

VERNON. Or a weddin' reception. He's caught more bride's bouquets than anyone in the village except Jewel.

KATE. Did he honestly think he went down on the Titanic?

VERNON. Caught that little fabrication, did you?

CRANE. (*Sits back on back of sofa.*) Kate catches everything, Verne.

VERNON. Well, the Colonel picks up any conversation and fits right in. Why, I've even heard him talk of bein' at Gettysburg and givin' that address.

CRANE. He actually thought he was Lincoln?

VERNON. T'weren't Queen Victoria. (*Dramatically strikes his Lincoln pose.*) "Four score and ten years ago—"

KATE. That's the one. I knew it sounded familiar.

VERNON. Ayah, beautiful words. Colonel picks up on the TV, too. After THE ELEPHANT MAN was on, he didn't walk straight for a month.

CRANE. If THE BOSTON STRANGLER comes on, we'll lock our doors.

VERNON. It's an insult to lock your doors.

KATE. That explains why I have so few friends in the city. (*PHONE rings.*)

CRANE. (*Rises.*) Who knows we're here?

VERNON. Mabel has spread the word.

KATE. (*Rises and speaks into phone.*) This is a recording. If you'll wait till the beep . . . Oh, Mabel, you recognized me . . . Yes, I'm just Jim-dandy. What can I do for you? . . . You found him. (*To* VERNON.) Verne, it's for you.

VERNON. (KATE *hands him the phone and goes to* CRANE.) Hope it's not a fire.

CRANE. You're a volunteer fireman, too?

VERNON. We all gotta help. (*Into phone. Tips hat.*) Verne here. How's the husband? . . . Ayah. And the children? . . . Ayah. And your Grandma?

CRANE. If it's a fire, it's now a pile of ashes.

VERNON. (*Into phone.*) Be right there. Thanks, Mabel. (*Starts to hang up, then back into phone.*) Say hello to your husband. and the children. (*Hangs up.*)

CRANE. You forgot Grandma.

VERNON. Don't do no good. Deaf as a gatepost. (*Goes to front door.*) Gotta go now. A car's parked by the fire hydrant in front of the General Store.

CRANE. (*Goes to him.*) Do your duty, Verne. Get right down there and give it a ticket.

VERNON. Nope.

CRANE. Why not?

VERNON. My car. (*Exits.* CRANE *closes the door and leans against it laughing.*)

KATE. And you came up here to work?

CRANE. I think we've taken care of all the bucolic problems. I am going to unpack and then I'll tell you my outline.

KATE. (*As goes to typewriter by stairs.*) If anyone else shows up I'm going to tell them we have Rocky Mountain Spotted Fever. I'll put my typewriter in the library till we need it.

CRANE. (*At stairs.*) It won't take me long to unpack. I didn't bring anything formal. (*Starts upstairs.*)

KATE. What about the square dance? Isn't it black tie? (*Exits into library.*)

CRANE. (*Comes back downstairs. To herself.*) I'm going to take these flowers to my room. (*Is picking them up when she sees the closet door opening slowly. She goes to it as* JOEL *backs out, his eyes towards the library. When she is behind him, she taps him on the shoulder. He jumps and turns.*)

JOEL. (*Puts his hand over her mouth.*) Quiet! Please! (CRANE *makes inaudible sounds.*)

KATE. (*Off Stage.*) Did you say something?

JOEL. Don't tell her I'm here. No one must know. No one. (*Goes into closet and closes door as* KATE *comes back Up* C.)

KATE. You're unpacked already?

CRANE. (*In a hollow voice.*) Not quite.

KATE. You look funny. Do you feel all right?

CRANE. Kate, you won't believe this.

KATE. Try me.

CRANE. There is a man in that closet.

KATE. You're right. I don't believe you.

CRANE. I'm having a deja vu. It's just like last time. It's back.

KATE. The same man?

CRANE. No, but the same closet.

KATE. You're putting me on.

CRANE. Open that door.

KATE. It's the air. You've been breathing too much of

it. I tell you it's too pure up here. You need those lovely little grimey New York particles in it.

CRANE. Just open that door.

KATE. And I'll see a man standing there?

CRANE. Uh-huh.

KATE. (*Crosses below* CRANE *to closet.*) And if I don't.

CRANE. (*Goes below her to closet.*) Then I shall marry the Colonel and settle down.

KATE. There is a man in there, you're sure? (CRANE *nods.* KATE *opens the door and* JOEL *is standing there. She closes the door.*) You're right, there is a man in there.

CRANE. What will we do?

KATE. Do you think Jewel can cope with another for dinner?

CRANE. We'd best see what he wants.

KATE. Wait a minute. (*Crosses to desk and picks up vase of flowers. Gives the flowers to* CRANE.) Here. Hold these. (*Goes to closet with vase held up.*) Just in case he's not collecting for the local Grange. (KATE *is to the* L. *of the closet and* CRANE *to the* R.) Open it.

CRANE. (*Opens closet door and it is empty.*) He's gone. (JOEL *comes in through Up* C. *and crosses to behind* KATE.)

KATE. We did see a man in there, didn't we?

CRANE. Definitely.

KATE. Then where is he?

CRANE. Turn around.

KATE. (*She does and* JOEL *is right behind her.*) Oh. You were just in that closet.

JOEL. I know.

CRANE. (*Acting the polite hostess.*) How do you do. I'm Crane Hammond and this is my secretary, Kate Bixley. (JOEL *puts out his hand,* CRANE *shakes.* KATE *goes to shake but has the vase in her hand.*)

JOEL. How do you do. I'm Joel Dover. Miss Bixley. (*They go to shake.*)

KATE. Sorry. (*Hands vase to* CRANE *who puts the flowers back in it.*) How do you do. (*They shake.*)

CRANE. Mr. Dover, are you going to leave or shall we call the police?

KATE. Sheriff Cookley is an intimate friend.

JOEL. I am the police.

CRANE. Good. Then we won't have to call you. (*Puts the vase on top shelf of what-not.*)

KATE. Do you have some identification?

JOEL. Not on me.

CRANE. The police have to carry ID's.

JOEL. Not when they're with the CIA on special assignment.

CRANE. (*Angry. Swings below sofa to below desk.*) That does it. Out. Out. Out. I'm not going to get involved. This happened to me last time I came here and I won't have it again. Kate, show Mr. Dover the door.

KATE. (*Pointing.*) That is the door.

JOEL. I must remain here.

KATE. Are you really from the CIA?

JOEL. Certainly. (*Goes to* CRANE.) And I might add, Mrs. Hammond, that I'm a devotee of your books. You have remarkable insight.

CRANE. You're trying to get around me.

KATE. And you're succeeding.

CRANE. (*Smiling modestly.*) Of course I do a lot of research so they sound authentic.

JOEL. Your scene with the files in SPIES OF THE PENTAGON was so realistic I could have sworn you worked there.

KATE. Crane, the police—

CRANE. Be quiet, Kate. (*To* JOEL, *smiling.*) Keep talking, Mr. Dover.

JOEL. And your characters. The realism. The way they speak, the way they think. The action is so realistic.

KATE. And I thought page 161 was overwritten.

CRANE. (*Sits at desk.*) And what can we do for you, Mr. Dover?

KATE. We can not get involved.

CRANE. I'm sure this nice gentleman wouldn't ask us to do anything wrong, would you?

JOEL. You must help me catch a spy.

CRANE. You see, Kate?

KATE. (*Crosses to* JOEL.) Crane has a whole book to write. Can't you catch him some place else?

JOEL. It's here at midnight. I wouldn't involve you but you did come a day early. You see, thirty days hath September—

KATE. We know that. Mr. Dover, can't you get someone else to help you?

JOEL. This is where it's going to happen.

KATE. Then we'll go somewhere else, won't we, Crane? Maybe Jewel is giving a slumber party.

CRANE. I won't leave. No foreign government is throwing me out of my house.

KATE. He might not be foreign.

CRANE. Spies are always foreign. He is foreign, isn't he, Mr. Dover?

JOEL. We're not sure. The spy who put us onto this spy, however, is Chester Grant from Fargo, North Dakota.

CRANE. Almost foreign, Kate. It't up near the Canadian border.

JOEL. Chester Grant is a double-agent.

CRANE. (*Rises and goes below desk to sofa.*) And you don't know where he is and he's going to show up here at midnight.

JOEL. It's amazing.

CRANE. You see, Kate, simple.

JOEL. It's amazing you're completely wrong. I thought you, at least, would know it's more complicated than that.

CRANE. Sorry. (*Sits.*)

JOEL. (*Goes to her.*) Chester Grant has been over there for years working in our Embassy.

KATE. By "over there", do you mean in—

CRANE. Kate! No names, please. Right, Mr. Dover?

JOEL. Absolutely. Grant was in our embassy there and under orders to allow himself to be blackmailed.

KATE. (*Crosses to* JOEL.) How did they do it?

CRANE. You know, Kate. Page 161.

KATE. Fascinating.

JOEL. (*Sits by* CRANE *on sofa.*) So they thought they had him blackmailed to turn over information to them. Naturally, Chester only turned over what we gave him.

CRANE. Some of it was authentic enough so they'd believe he was working for them, right?

JOEL. I knew you would finally understand. That brings us up to the present.

KATE. (*Moves above sofa.*) Midnight tonight?

JOEL. Precisely. For years Chester has infiltrated himself further and further into their confidence until he managed to gain access to their—

CRANE. Don't tell me. Access to their list of agents in this country?

JOEL. Afraid not.

KATE. (*Crosses to* R. *of sofa.*) You can't hit them all or I'd send you to Las Vegas.

JOEL. What Chester got was access to all their military installations.

CRANE. If I could interview him, I'd have a best-seller.

JOEL. I only wish *I* could interview him.

KATE. He's disappeared?

JOEL. More or less.

CRANE. Which is it — more or less?

JOEL. Chester left — er — "over there", but by the time he arrived here he was missing.

CRANE. With the information.

JOEL. A brilliant agent.

KATE. (*Sits in chair Down* R.) He doesn't sound it.

JOEL. He had the whole thing reduced to a microdot no bigger than a period on a typewriter.

CRANE. And he put it over a period in a book he was carrying?

JOEL. Wrong again.

CRANE. But they always do that.

JOEL. Chester was more ingenious. He put it on his face so it looked like a mole.

CRANE. Kate, make notes of this.

KATE. I won't forget a word, believe me.

JOEL. When we found him after he'd been attacked —

CRANE. I thought he'd disappeared.

JOEL. His body is with us but not his mind.

CRANE. Where is that?

JOEL. Somewhere, but not here. It's coming back day by day.

CRANE. But the microdot mole is gone?

JOEL. You're right.

KATE. Bingo!

CRANE. Whoever attacked him has it?

JOEL. Oh, we know where it is.

CRANE. Where?

JOEL. When he was brought into the hospital in New York City—

KATE. I love that place.

JOEL. Naturally, the nurse cleaned him up and the mole ended up stuck to some cotton in the garbage.

CRANE. Lost forever.

KATE. (*Excited, she rises and goes to* R. *of sofa.*) No, no, it wasn't, was it, Mr. Dover? Tell her it wasn't.

JOEL. It wasn't.

CRANE. But why not?

KATE. (*With a smile.*) Bless that rotten city of mine. There was a garbage strike.

JOEL. And it took three days for the microdot to be found.

KATE. (*Sits on the* R. *sofa arm.*) Then your problems are solved.

JOEL. Not quite.

CRANE. Kate, he said the microdot was found but he didn't say our side found it.

KATE. Oh, no!

JOEL. Oh, yes! Due to the strike, all trash cans were stored in the basement of City Hospital. That's where it was found and guess where he brought it.

CRANE AND KATE. Right here!

JOEL. Correct. It was delivered to the man who rented this house last month.

KATE. It's still this month. Thirty days hath September, remember?

JOEL. This month.

CRANE. You said it was delivered?

JOEL. (*Rises and goes* C.) We picked up the trail of the doctor who took the microdot. We've had him under surveillance for years. Supposedly defected here but we knew better.

KATE. Good for our side.

JOEL. He suddenly said he was vacationing here in Vermont, but we had found his fingerprints on that trash can.

CRANE. So you knew better.

JOEL. He brought the microdot here and turned it over to the renter of this house to be sent onto the other side. His job done, he returned to the hospital and, as of ten o'clock this morning, he was performing a double by-pass on an opera singer.

CRANE. How do you know he left it here?

JOEL. (*Sits in chair* C.) This village has been a shipping-off place for material to the other side ever since World War Two. Whoever the master spy is, he lives here. His cover is perfect.

CRANE. Then how are you going to uncover him?

JOEL. Capitalism wins again. The go-between who rented this house was ordered back home the end of the year. He couldn't face giving up all our luxuries; his Thunderbird, his closet full of double-breasted Brooks Brothers suits and Calvin Klein jeans, the movies, the television —

KATE. He was probably hooked on DALLAS.

CRANE. To say nothing of our fine restaurants.

KATE. (*Between sofa and chair.*) Imagine a land with no McDonalds.

JOEL. He defected and told us all.

CRANE. Exactly what was all?

JOEL. He knows that on midnight, the last day of the month, all deliveries are picked up here. The microdot will be taken from this house at the stroke of midnight tonight.

CRANE. But where is it?

JOEL. Ah, there's the rub.

KATE. I knew there'd be a rub.

CRANE. There always is, Kate, or there'd be no story. Tell us the rub, Mr. Dover.

JOEL. Just as the go-between was going to say where the microdot was, he gasped and dropped dead.

CRANE. Cyanide.

JOEL. Twelve pieces of cheesecake at Lindy's. He'd been celebrating.

KATE. He should have joined Weight Watchers. (*Goes to desk.*)

CRANE. (*Rises.*) So you want us to go somewhere till after midnight tonight. You pick up the microdot and the master spy.

JOEL. You can't go now.

CRANE. Why not?

JOEL. Everyone in town knows you're here. If you leave, it will look suspicious and the spy won't show up.

CRANE. Everyone doesn't know we're here.

JOEL. Mabel knows.

KATE. Then everyone does know.

CRANE. What are we supposed to do when he comes, offer him a drink and tell him to pick up his microdot?

JOEL. He—

KATE. Or she. Always say, "He or she". Crane does in all her books, don't you?

CRANE. Always. It confuses the reader.

JOEL. When the spy, whatever sex it is, comes, he obviously won't pick up the plans if you're watching him. You should go to bed, leave the coast clear.

CRANE. (*Goes to* JOEL.) Suppose the plans are in the bedroom? There's no telling what he might do.

KATE. (*With a leer.*) That's true. Page 161. Oh, Crane, he—

CRANE. Or she, remember?

KATE. There goes that fantasy.

JOEL. (*Crosses below sofa.*) We must assume the microdot is easily accessible for a quick entrance and exit.

KATE. Perhaps we could find it.

CRANE. Kate, do you know how many dots there are in each of those books, (*Crosses Down C.*) let alone elsewhere—the carpet, the sofa, the desk drawers?

JOEL. It must be somewhere very safe.

KATE. But where? (*PHONE RINGS.* KATE *rises.*)

CRANE. I'll get it. It might be Richard. (*Goes to phone.*)

KATE. (*Crosses below desk and to* JOEL.) That's her husband. He's an author, too. Philosophical novels.

CRANE. He's an excellent writer.

KATE. Hasn't hit the top ten.

CRANE. (*Into phone.*) Hello . . . yes, it is . . . what? . . . who is this? . . . how much? . . . twenty thousand dollars?

KATE. Goody, it's her agent. (*Sits on sofa.*)

CRANE. (*Into phone.*) But I'm not who you think I am . . .

KATE. It's not her agent. He knows her very well.

CRANE. (*Into phone.*) I don't know anything about any military installations . . . (JOEL *rises and goes above sofa.*) You can call later, but I still won't know, and I am not a spy! . . . Hello, hello . . .

JOEL. Who was it? Did you recognize his voice?

CRANE. (*Sits at desk with a shocked look.*) I just turned down twenty thousand dollars.

KATE. It would have put you in a higher tax bracket.

JOEL. (*Goes above desk.*) What did he say?

KATE. He or she?

CRANE. I couldn't tell, the voice was very muffled. But he or she offered me all that money for the plans. He said he'd be in touch later.

KATE. (*Rises.*) You talked to the master spy.

CRANE. No, it wasn't him. He knows where the plans are.

JOEL. If the go-between told him. We're not sure. No, that call was someone offering to buy them.

CRANE. That's two people who know.

KATE. More than two.

CRANE. What do you mean? (KATE *points at phone.*) Of course. Mabel.

KATE. By now, she's telling all her intimates that something up here is worth twenty thousand dollars.

CRANE. Maybe she knows who the call came from. (*Picks up phone.*)

JOEL. (*Moves Down* C.) He's too smart for that.

CRANE. Mabel . . . Mabel . . . (*Jiggles receiver.*) You're right. She's spreading the word already. (*Into phone.*) Oh, there you are, Mabel . . . yes, a nice relaxing day . . . Mabel, I had a call just now. (*Covers mouthpiece.*) She's acting surprised.

KATE. (*Goes to* JOEL.) That's worth an Academy Award.

CRANE. (*Into phone.*) Mabel, did you happen to hear who it was? . . . No, no, you wouldn't eavesdrop . . . No, I—I—

KATE. Methinks the lady doth protest too much.

CRANE. (*Into phone.*) I just wondered if you would know where the call came from?

JOEL. (*To* KATE.) A pay booth.

CRANE. (*Into phone.*) A pay booth? Did you recognize the voice?

JOEL. (*To* KATE.) It was disguised.

CRANE. (*Into phone.*) It was disguised?

KATE. (*To* JOEL.) Say, you're good.

JOEL. Thank you.

CRANE. (*Into phone.*) No, nothing important. I think

it was my publisher giving me some ideas for a story. Good-bye, Mabel. (*Hangs up.*)

KATE. She'll never swallow that.

CRANE. Who could it have been?

JOEL. Almost anyone in town.

CRANE. No one knows about the microdot but us.

JOEL. Mrs. Hammond, you're a very good writer of suspense and spies but you're very naive.

KATE. You haven't read page 161.

JOEL. If we know this is a pick-up spot for information, others know it as well.

CRANE. You mean some other country?

JOEL. Our own. It's that rotten FBI.

KATE. Don't you work together?

KATE. (*Crosses away below sofa.*) Good God, no. We're two distinct branches and the jealousy is unparalleled.

KATE. (*Goes towards him.*) For the sake of the country, can't you bury the hatchet and ask them what they know?

JOEL. (*Sinks on sofa.*) They wouldn't tell us. We'd be the butt of every joke in Washington. Their P. R. department would have a field day with us.

CRANE. How would they have found out about the plans?

JOEL. They spy. Damned good, too. They have double agents in our office and, let me add, we have them in theirs.

KATE. You spy on each other?

JOEL. Of course.

CRANE. (*Rises and goes below desk.*) Then we have one master spy from over there and possibly one internal spy from over here. What are we going to do?

JOEL. There's nothing we can do but wait till midnight.

KATE. (*Above sofa.*) Suppose no one shows up?
JOEL. They will. (*KNOCK on door.*)
KATE. They have.
JOEL. (*Rises and goes by chair* C.) I mustn't be seen here.
CRANE. Why not?
JOEL. You two are known to be here. I'm not. We mustn't arouse any more suspicions than are here already.
CRANE. (*Crosses to* JOEL *and pushes him Up* C.) Go into the library.
JOEL. Try to find out if they know anything. Be clever.
KATE. (*Goes to* L. *of* CRANE.) Clever? This is Crane Hammond.
JOEL. And this is life. (*The front door opens and* LYDIA SCOTT *is there. She is middle-aged, a bit fussy and overwrought at times. She is dressed in a comfortable Summer dress and carries a purse.*)
LYDIA. Anyone home? (*Since* CRANE *and* JOEL *are to the* R. *of the door, only* KATE *is visible to* LYDIA. CRANE *pushes* JOEL *into library.*)
KATE. Everyone. (*Decides on a gushing attack to distract* LYDIA.) How do you do. So nice of you to drop by. Can I do anything for you?
LYDIA. How nice you are.
KATE. Why, thank you.
LYDIA. I was almost afraid to open the door. I understand New Yorkers shoot first and ask questions afterwards.
KATE. No, that's the Old West.
LYDIA. Actually, I am looking for Crane Hammond. Are you she?
KATE. No. I am not she. She is there. (LYDIA *turns as* CRANE *closes the door.*)

LYDIA. Mrs. Hammond, this is such a great pleasure.
CRANE. Do come in.
LYDIA. Thank you. I do wish we could meet under more normal circumstances.
CRANE. Like what?
LYDIA. Like my not having to ask for you-know-what.
CRANE. I'm afraid I don't know what.
LYDIA. (*With a little laugh.*) Oh, yes you do. Come now, think.
KATE. I think you do know what, Crane.
LYDIA. I have to get it before midnight.
CRANE. But you're going to give me something in exchange?
LYDIA. You already have it. Isn't the house satisfactory?
CRANE. The house? It's just lovely.
LYDIA. (*Sits in chair* C.) Now about the money—
CRANE. Yes, the money. (*Sits on the sofa.*)
LYDIA. If you divide the rent by thirty-one—
CRANE. The rent?
LYDIA. That's fair, isn't it?
CRANE. (*Starts laughing.*) Oh, you're Lydia Whatever, the real estate lady.
LYDIA. Yes, Lydia Scott.
CRANE. We thought you were . . . (*Stops laughing and sobers up.*) I'm terribly sorry.
KATE. (*Sits on the back of the desk.*) We were testing out some of Mrs. Hammond's new dialogue. We wanted to see how it would sound.
LYDIA. So that's the way you work. How exciting.
KATE. A thrill a minute.
CRANE. Mrs. Scott—Miss Scott?
LYDIA. It's Ms. but why don't you call me Lydia?

CRANE. (*Smiles.*) I can't think of any reason why not. Lydia, we came a day early by mistake—
LYDIA. Yes. You forgot. Thirty days hath September—
CRANE. That's one thing we have remembered.
KATE. I'll just pop into the library and get my checkbook and give you one day's extra rent. (*Starts for library.*)
CRANE. And see if everything is all right in there.
KATE. Got you. (*Exits.*)
LYDIA. I must admit I've come here with an ulterior motive. Several of them.
CRANE. Well, let's take them one at a time.
LYDIA. (*Crosses and sits by* CRANE *of sofa.*) Fine. I also write a society column for the paper. Naturally, I want to do a full article on you later but, for the moment, can I just have a quote, something titillating? (*Takes pad and pencil from purse.*)
CRANE. About what?
LYDIA. Let me ask you a leading question. Do you like our village? (KATE *rushes in from the library with her briefcase and puts it on the desk. She waves her arms at* CRANE *and signals that* JOEL *is not in the library.*)
CRANE. (*To* KATE.) What! (KATE *continues saying* JOEL *is gone.*)
LYDIA. Do you like our village?
CRANE. (*Understand* KATE's *gestures.*) Oh, my God, no!
LYDIA. I can't quote you on that. I restrict my column to happy news.
CRANE. Pardon me.
LYDIA. I can't say you don't like it here.
CRANE. But I do. I do. (KATE *waits nervously. To*

her.) It's so much better than being *closeted* up in the city.

KATE. Oh, closet.

LYDIA. (*Sees* KATE *for the first time.*) I beg your pardon.

KATE. I was just agreeing with Crane. New York is just one big closet.

LYDIA. (*To* CRANE.) Then you do like it here?

CRANE. Of course. (KATE *goes to the closet.*)

LYDIA. Say something quotable, please. (*Her pencil is poised.*)

CRANE. (*Her attention on* KATE *who opens the closet.* JOEL *is standing there. He waves and* KATE *closes the door, returns to the desk and writes the check.*) These hills are alive with the sound of music.

LYDIA. Oh, that's good. That's very good. (*Writing.*) . . . alive with the . . . (*Looks up.*) What kind of music?

CRANE. Sound. Sound of music.

LYDIA. Yes. (*Finishes writing.*)

CRANE. And what other ulterior motive do you have, Lydia?

LYDIA. What? Oh, yes. (*Pad and pencil back in purse.*) The annual Church Fair is next week and I wonder if we could impose on you to autograph some of your books for us?

CRANE. I'd be delighted.

LYDIA. They'll get a good price. (*Rises and goes Up* C.) We have three in the library and I have one of my own. A complete one, if you know what I mean.

CRANE. I'm afraid I don't.

LYDIA. The library board are such fuffy-duddies. They took a pair of garden shears to page 161. Mine is intact.

CRANE. (*Crosses to her.*) You're a liberated woman, Lydia.

LYDIA. I like to think so.

KATE. (*Goes to* LYDIA *with check.*) Here you are. Paid in full.

LYDIA. Thanks so much. (CRANE *opens front door.*) I'll get those books and would it be asking too much for you to sign six copies of THE SPY WHO TRIED?

CRANE. Of course not. I didn't know there was still such interest in my first book.

LYDIA. It will be the hit of White Elephant table. (*Exits.*)

CRANE. (*As she closes the door.*) It's come to that.

KATE. Perhaps they'll become collector's items like the original Superman.

CRANE. (*As she goes to the closet.*) I always read Wonder Woman. (*Opens door.* JOEL *is there.*) It's good you don't get claustrophobia.

JOEL. (*Comes out.*) It's part of our training. All clear now?

CRANE. That was just one of the locals calling.

JOEL. Beware of the locals.

CRANE. Not Lydia Scott. She's just—

JOEL. Training, Mrs. Hammond, they're trained by experts, too. (*Goes to windows and looks out cautiously.*) The least likely person is our master spy.

KATE. Then it is obviously Vernon Cookley.

CRANE. Not Verne.

JOEL. (*Turns.*) You mustn't say "not anyone". It could be, and it is, someone perfectly ordinary.

KATE. Then it isn't Verne.

JOEL. (*Goes below sofa.*) One of the toughest cases we ever cracked turned up the spy as an eight year old child prodigy.

CRANE. (*Crosses down.*) An eight year old spy?

JOEL. Midget. Actually forty-three. She played the bass viola standing on a small stool. We closed in just before her Times Hall debut. Had to refund all the tickets.

KATE. (*Shudders, sits at desk.*) Oh, the bookkeeping.

JOEL. Naturally, no one minded talking in front of her. She gleaned information from the most unlkikely sources with her childish wiles. You'll never guess where we found the film of our latest missiles.

KATE. In the plastic barrette holding back her golden curls?

JOEL. No.

CRANE. In her yo-yo?

JOEL. How did you know that?

CRANE. I write these characters, all sorts from sweet children to drunkards.

KATE. Ah, a drink. Isn't it time?

CRANE. It's way after. (*Goes to the bar.*) What would you like, Mr. Dover?

JOEL. (*Sits on the sofa.*) Never drink on duty. Perhaps there's something non-alcoholic.

CRANE. Not even a Diet Pepsi.

KATE. (*Goes to kitchen door.*) I'll case the kitchen. If I'm lucky, I'll find some grape juice or maybe even gooseberry Kool-Aid. (*Exits.*)

CRANE. (*Opens Scotch bottle, then calls after* KATE.) Oh, Kate—(*Realizes she is gone. To* JOEL.) Maybe you could help her get some ice?

JOEL. No trouble.(*Goes towards kitchen.*)

CRANE. And we need some water. (*Starts towards him with pitcher.*)

JOEL. Right you are. (*Turns at kitchen door.*)

KATE. (*She enters.*) You'll need some water. (*Swings door open and it hits* JOEL *in the back as he has turned to* CRANE. *A sound of pain from* JOEL *and he collapses towards* CRANE.) Oh, sorry. Did I—

CRANE. Joel! (*He continues hopping about with "Owws" and "Ohhs".*)

KATE. Oh, no! Are you all right?

CRANE. (*Puts pitcher back on desk.*) Of course he's not all right. You smacked him on the back.

JOEL. (*Rubbing his head.*) My head! Owww, my head!

CRANE. Ice. Kate, get ice.

KATE. We'll need it for the drinks anyway. (*Goes to kitchen.*)

CRANE. (*Her arm around* JOEL, *she leads him to the sofa.*) Rub it. That's the best thing. Keep rubbing it.

JOEL. I am. I'm rubbing myself bald. (CRANE *sits him on the sofa, remains to his* R.)

CRANE. Maybe you should put your feet up.

JOEL. My feet don't hurt. It's my head and that's up already.

CRANE. Here, let me look. (*Takes his hands away from his head.*) I see a bump. Right there. (*Puts her finger on it.*)

JOEL. Ouch!

CRANE. Yes, that's it.

JOEL. I know it.

CRANE. It's not bleeding though. (*Sits to his* R.) You'll be all right in a minute.

JOEL. I think it knocked my teeth loose.

CRANE. Are they your own?

JOEL. What?

CRANE. Your teeth. Are they yours?

JOEL. Yes, but my eyes aren't. Contact lenses.

CRANE. Are they still in?

JOEL. Wait till I focus. (*Holds three fingers in front of himself and moves them back and forth.*)

CRANE. How many fingers do you see?

JOEL. I know the answer. I'm holding them up. (*Looks carefully.*) Clear as a bell. The lenses are in.

CRANE. Good. Anything else loose?

JOEL. Everything else is mine.

KATE. (*Comes in with ice wrapped in kitchen towel.*) Ice coming up.

CRANE. He'll live.

JOEL. I'm glad you think so.

KATE. (*Standing by him.*) Where will I put it?

CRANE. Give it to me. (*Rises and takes wrapped ice.*) Now I'll put it right here. (*Puts it on JOEL's head rather roughly. He yelps.*)

JOEL. Perhaps I'd better do it. (*Takes it and gingerly places it on his head, puts his hands down and looks at them. KATE laughs.*) What's so funny?

KATE. I'm really very sorry.

JOEL. You don't sound it.

KATE. You look so silly.

JOEL. I don't feel silly, Miss — er —

KATE. Bixley.

JOEL. Bixley. Yes. Perhaps I should have a drink.

CRANE. You said you didn't drink on duty.

JOEL. What duty?

CRANE. Your duty? Here. Now.

JOEL. Oh. Yes, of course. But I'm sure a straight Scotch will clear my mind.

KATE. Right. (*Goes to bar and pours drink.*)

CRANE. (*Sits by him.*) Is your mind fuzzy?

JOEL. A bit rattled, that's all. Everything's jumbled up. Got to straighten it out.

CRANE. I got hit with a baseball once when I was eight years old.

JOEL. Was your mind fuzzy?

CRANE. Not at all.
KATE. (*Crossing back with drink.*) Then why did you bring it up?
CRANE. It hurt and I'm sympathizing with him.
KATE. Drink this. We won't snitch on you. (*He downs it in one swallow.*)
CRANE. There, now, all better?
JOEL. I have a cold chill down my back.
CRANE. (*Looks.*) That's just the ice melting.
KATE. I'll get a dry towel.
JOEL. Thanks, but I don't think I need any more.
KATE. (*Takes towel.*) Then I'll take it back to the kitchen. Anything else I can do for you? (*Starts for the kitchen.*)
JOEL. Yes. Tell me exactly what I am doing here. (KATE *freezes at kitchen door, turns slowly back.* CRANE *rises.*)
CRANE. What you're doing here?
KATE. (*Sensing disaster.*) Oh, dear me!
JOEL. I mean I know I'm here, of course, and it's lovely. The view and the house and you two ladies, but as far as anything else goes, I'm a bit muddy.
CRANE. Exactly how muddy? Just a little bit —
KATE. Or like the whole Okefenokee Swamp?
CRANE. Do you know who I am?
JOEL. Not really.
KATE. How about me?
JOEL. Definitely not.
CRANE. How about yourself?
JOEL. Naturally, I know I am me. I mean, here I am.
CRANE. Yes, there you are.
KATE. You definitely are there.
JOEL. But I can't think of my name and I don't know

what I'm doing here. It's the bump on my head. I'm rattled. I assume one of you is my wife but I'm not sure which one.

KATE. (*After exchanging a look with* CRANE.) Take your pick.

JOEL. Well, I choose — (*Front door opens and* JEWEL *bounds in with a large bag filled with groceries.*)

JEWEL. Supper's here.

JOEL. (*Rises.*) Not her, I hope.

JEWEL. Didn't know we was expectin' company. Have to stretch supper.

CRANE. (*Rises.*) Jewel, we didn't tell you about this gentleman.

JEWEL. That's right. You didn't.

KATE. And we shouldn't.

JEWEL. No skin off my nose.

KATE. He said we shouldn't tell anyone.

JOEL. I did?

CRANE. But, Kate, under the circumstances —

KATE. No!

CRANE. Well, I'm going to. (*To* JEWEL.) Jewel, this is —

KATE. This is Crane's husband.

CRANE. What!

JEWEL. How do.

JOEL. My wife? (*Throws arms around* CRANE.) I would have picked you anyway.

CURTAIN

ACT TWO

Scene 1.

(*Evening, the same day.* CRANE *is sitting on the chair* C., JOEL *is on the sofa. Coffee service is on the desk.* KATE *has poured coffee for* JOEL *and* CRANE *and is crossing to them.*)

CRANE. You did very well at dinner, Joel.
KATE. (*Hands coffee to* CRANE.) Richard. Your husband's name is Richard.
CRANE. I know that.
JOEL. I wish you two would make up your mind. First you tell me I'm Joel and then you call me Richard. (*Takes coffee from* KATE.)
KATE. Just answer to anything masculine.
JOEL. Maybe this coffee will straighten me out. (KATE *goes to desk and pours herself coffee.*)
CRANE. If two shots of Scotch didn't, I wouldn't bank on Jewel's Instant Folgers.
JOEL. (*Taps his head.*) It's like a jig-saw puzzle up here. I can't get it together.
CRANE. Start with the outside and then fill in the middle. That's what I always do.
JOEL. You start telling me everything about Joel and then that Jewel woman strides in and you talk to me as Richard. It is very confusing.
CRANE. You are Joel but we have to call you Richard in front of Jewel so she won't know—
KATE. (*Crosses by* JOEL.)—that you really are Joel.
CRANE. And not my husband, Richard.

KATE. And, as Joel, you're working undercover for the government.

CRANE. Until midnight when you capture a master spy.

KATE. And you won't have to be Richard any more.

CRANE. You can be Joel permanently.

KATE. And that's it in a nutshell.

JOEL. I must say I sound very clever. I feel very clever, too. If only I knew what I'm being clever about.

CRANE. At midnight a spy is picking up some important information here and you're going to apprehend him.

JOEL. But who is he?

CRANE. You don't know that yet.

KATE. (*Crosses above desk and sits in desk chair.*) And neither do we.

JOEL. And I can't let him see me because, if he does, he'll know what I'm doing here?

KATE. So, to satisfy Jewel, we call you Crane's husband.

JOEL. Richard?

KATE. Yes.

JOEL. What will we do at midnight?

CRANE. We haven't gotten that far yet.

JOEL. Just one question.

CRANE. What?

JOEL. If the spy could be anyone, then why not the most obvious?

KATE. You mean Vernon Cookley?

JOEL. No.

CRANE. Who, then?

JOEL. Me.

CRANE. (*She and* KATE *exchange a look as* KATE *rises.*) I never thought of that.

KATE. (*Goes to* JOEL.) You're good, Joel. You're really very good. See how your deductive mind works. You're getting better.

JOEL. If I incriminate myself, is that getting better?

CRANE. It couldn't be you because you told us all about the plot and you didn't have to.

JOEL. Unless I thought it would trap you if either of you is the master spy.

CRANE. That's a good point, isn't it, Kate?

KATE. Crane, you couldn't — you wouldn't —

CRANE. Of course I wouldn't, but, if I were you, I wouldn't mention just returning from a trip to the Capitols of Europe.

JOEL. You did that?

KATE. Yes, but —

CRANE. And she never took one American Express Tour to any points of interest.

JOEL. Hmmm.

KATE. (*To* CRANE.) Who's side are you on?

JEWEL. (*Comes from kitchen carrying a plate of eight chocolate chip cookies.*) Here's dessert. Don't blame me.

KATE. (*Taking one, feigning delight.*) You made them yourself.

JEWEL. I was plannin' on a quick-bake maple layer cake but there was only one quarter cup of flour left.

KATE. Chocolate chip. My favorite. (*Bites one.*)

JEWEL. Home made.

KATE. You're sure that was flour and not plaster of Paris? (*Sits at desk with coffee.*)

JEWEL. I didn't bake them. They was in the kitchen. (*Goes above sofa and* CRANE *takes one.*)

KATE. Then the former tenant didn't read THE JOY OF COOKING.

JEWEL. (*Crosses below sofa and offers one to* JOEL *who takes it.*) He was an odd one. Besides these, he left those candy bars and a can of Borscht, whatever that is, a tin of them black fish eggs —
KATE. Caviar?
JEWEL. I reckon, and there's three bottles of Vodka where cans of food oughta be.
JOEL. Borscht, caviar, and Vodka. Traces of the old country.
JEWEL. And, besides the cookies, frozen fish sticks, frozen waffles, and an empty container of Colonel Sanders' fried chicken.
CRANE. (*To* JOEL.) You're right. He was turning American.
JEWEL. I don't hold with them foreign foods.
KATE. I could tell dinner was frozen right here in the good old U.S. of A.
JEWEL. Didn't have time for nothin' else. Tomorrow, we'll really dig in.
JOEL. This cookie really is very interesting.
KATE. I think Toll House should sue for doing this to a chocolate chip.
JEWEL. (*Goes between chair and desk.*) Tomorrow I'll bake some from my own recipe. They got in the village cook book. Called the Jewel's Jawbreakers.
CRANE. Sounds delicious.
KATE. Are they like hard tack?
JEWEL. Got ginger and cinnamon and walnuts and a touch of apple rind.
KATE. No Vermont maple syrup?
JEWEL. You pour that on top. Put one of them in your mouth and you can gum it around most of a full mornin'. (*Puts cookies on desk.*) Well, I gotta do the dishes. Lotta work.

EXIT WHO?

CRANE. Is the dishwasher broken?
JEWEL. You think I'd use one of them things?
KATE. Yes.
JEWEL. (*Glowering down on her.*) You do?
KATE. No, of course not.
JEWEL. My sister put her good company china in one of them things and it washed the flowers right off.
CRANE. Noritake?
JEWEL. No, Nancy. My youngest sister. Took her ages to collect that china. Got once piece a week at the A&P for five months.
JOEL. Could I have another cookie, please?
JEWEL. (*Passes cookies to him.*) It's your stomach.
CRANE. (*To* JOEL.) You'll need some Pepto-Bismol.
JOEL. I never get indigestion.
CRANE. Do you remember for sure?
JOEL. (*Happily.*) Yes, I do remember.
KATE. Good for you.
CRANE. It's marvelous. You do remember.
JEWEL. I don't think it's so great. (*Cookies on desk.*)
KATE. He's always eating things that don't agree with him and never remembers till afterwards, do you, Joel?
JOEL. That's right.
JEWEL. I thought your name was Richard.
CRANE. It it. Richard Joel Hammond.
KATE. Great authors always have three names.
JEWEL. Ayah, that's right. He's like Louisa May Alcott. (*Goes into kitchen.*)
JOEL. LITTLE WOMEN. See, I remember everything but the important things.
CRANE. Do you think if we hit you with another door everything would come back?
KATE. I don't mind doing it again.
JOEL. I do. It might knock the rest of my memory out.

CRANE. We can't have that. What can we do?

KATE. Let's play a game.

CRANE. (*Crosses to desk and puts cup down.*) Kate, this is no time for games. Besides I don't know if there are any cards here.

KATE. Not cards. Word association.

CRANE. (*Takes* JOEL'S *cup to desk.*) Of course, that will help him. Do you remember playing that, Joel?

JOEL. No.

CRANE. I say a word and then you say the first thing that comes into your head.

KATE. It will come from deep in your subconscience.

JOEL. What if I say something naughty?

KATE. We'll forgive you.

JOEL. Let me see how it works first. You do it.

CRANE. All right. Now, I'll say a word and Kate will say the first thing that pops into her head. Ready?

KATE. Shoot.

CRANE. Here goes. (*To* KATE.) Book.

KATE. Money.

JOEL. That's an odd association.

CRANE. The average person would say something like, "read".

JOEL. That's what I would have said.

CRANE. Good. I'll try another. (*To* KATE.) Right.

KATE. Money.

CRANE. Most people would say "wrong".

KATE. I thought you meant "write". W - r - i - t - e.

CRANE. Oh, Kate. Once more. Telephone.

KATE. Money.

CRANE. Really?

KATE. That reminded me I haven't paid my phone bill.

JOEL. I would say Miss Bixley has a one track mind.

KATE. It will work better on you.
CRANE. Ready, Joel?
JOEL. I'm ready.
CRANE. (*Fires the following words at him quickly and suddenly. He responds immediately. She goes below him to his R., turns suddenly.*) Man.
JOEL. Woman.
CRANE. Very good.
JOEL. (*Pleased with himself.*) Thank you. It just came to my mind.
CRANE. Black.
JOEL. White.
CRANE. Eat.
JOEL. Could I have another cookie, please? (*Goes to cookies on desk and takes one.*)
KATE. That was the first thing that came into your mind?
JOEL. Sorry, but I still feel hungry. That frozen Hawaiian dinner didn't quite fill me up. Go ahead, this is fun.
CRANE. Job.
JOEL. (*With mouth full.*) Work.
CRANE. What?
JOEL. Work. My mouth is full of chocolate chips.
CRANE. Swallow it. (*Waits while he does, sits on C. sofa arm.*) Government.
JOEL. "Of the people and for the people".
KATE. That's very patriotic but not very helpful.
CRANE. Spy.
JOEL. Who?
CRANE. No, spy.
JOEL. (*Moves in C.*) Who. That's my answer. Who.
CRANE. That's what we want to know. Who? (JOEL *sits in chair C.*)

KATE. (*Rises and goes to him.*) Let me try. Dot.
JOEL. Lamour.
KATE. How romantic, but what's it mean?
JOEL. Dotty Lamour in those sarong movies.
KATE. Military installations.
JOEL. (*Rises excitedly.*) Where are they? Have you got them?
CRANE. (*Rises.*) Got what?
JOEL. What did I say?
KATE. Who are you?
JOEL. Richard Hammond. No, Joel Dover. No — oh, I don't know. I almost had it.
CRANE. You reacted beautifully to military installaitons.
JOEL. Did I? Yes, I did. I jumped up. Now, why was that?
CRANE. You were remembering about the microdot.
JOEL. The one you say has the important information? I'll just have to take your word for it. I don't remember a thing.
CRANE. (*Goes to below sofa.*) We'll try again later.
JOEL. Maybe if I could lie down. It's very tiring trying to remember who you are.
CRANE. That's a good idea. A few minutes rest and everything will come popping back. (*Goes to windows and looks out.*) Kate, show Joel to the guest room.
KATE. (*Takes him by the arm to the stairs.*) Come along now. A little nap and we'll play another game later.
JOEL. Maybe I'll take an aspirin. No, Bufferin. See, I'm remembering.
CRANE. (*As the others go upstairs.*) Hurry back, Kate.
KATE. Right.
JOEL. Wrong.

KATE. That's very good, but we weren't playing. (*They are off.*)

CRANE. (*Looks at her watch.*) Three hours to find a dot. I know, the label of the Scotch bottle. (*Goes to the bar.*) No luck, but since I'm here—(*Pours a drink, ice from bucket and water from pitcher. She takes a swallow. Meanwhile,* CYRUS D. CONWAY *has appeared at the windows. He is a middle-aged man who is a go-getter and his drive is always evident.*)

CYRUS. Don't move!

CRANE. (*With her back to him.*) I won't. My purse is upstairs but I'd better warn you I take Karate.

CYRUS. Marvelous. You're just as I imagined, hard drinking and full of guts.

CRANE. (*Puts drink down.*) Can I turn around?

CYRUS. Do so and meet Cyrus D. Conway.

CRANE. (*Turns.*) I hate people who say things like, "You mean *the* Cyrus D. Conway?" but are you *the* Cyrus D. Conway?

CYRUS. (*Moves Up* C.) Every inch of me. And I have come to meet *the* Crane Hammond.

CRANE. But you're a recluse. Why aren't you reclusing?

CYRUS. Don't believe everything you read in the Enquirer. I do my business from home, it's true, but when I want something I go out and get it and I want you, Crane Hammond.

CRANE. For anything in particular?

CYRUS. For your words, those golden words that are brought forth from your typewriter by those flying fingers.

CRANE. My secretary does that. (*Goes to below desk.*) If you could see my typing you'd know why my flying fingers are grounded.

CYRUS. (*Goes to her.*) I am going to publish your

next book. When you hear the campaign I have laid out for you—

CRANE. I have an agent, Mr. Conway. Perhaps you should—

CYRUS. I don't bother with underlings. I go straight to the source. (*Moves away Down* C.) When I want a Toyota, I go to Tokyo, when I want a case of Perrier, I go to France. (*Turns and points at* CRANE.) And now I want you.

CRANE. You sound like Uncle Sam.

CYRUS. As you must know, among my many companies is Conway Publishing, which I immodestly admit is the third largest in world.

CRANE. I'm aware of that, but—

CYRUS. I am going to take your next book, Mrs. Hammond, and give you not only a first class printing but guarantee you a motion picture with a cast of thousands, and a TV series. (*Goes to her.*) Before I am through with you, Masterpiece Theatre will come begging.

CRANE. (*Getting her drink.*) I don't need anyone to beg for me, Mr. Conway. (*Leans across desk to him.*) I must insist that all negotiations go through my agent. He handled my first book and I am very loyal.

CYRUS. There is no loyalty where the dollar is concerned, to say nothing of the Yen, the Mark, and the Swiss Franc.

CRANE. (*Crosses below desk.*) My agent—I have a contract.

CYRUS. Contracts, like marriages, were made to be broken.

CRANE. (*Crosses below sofa.*) I bet you read that somewhere.

CYRUS. My publishing company needs a best-seller.

Ian Flemming is gone but you are here. (*Crosses to* c.) I'll have you know I don't drop everything and leave my compound for something trivial.

CRANE. (*Sits on sofa.*) What about the Toyota and the Perrier?

CYRUS. I will advance you any amount.

CRANE. How about—?

CYRUS. Within reason, of course.

CRANE. It's not for me to reason why.

CYRUS. Precisely. (*A loud CRASH comes from the kitchen.*) What's that?

CRANE. A tinkling piano in the next apartment.

CYRUS. (*Goes to her.*) Someone else is here.

CRANE. A few people do drop in now and then.

CYRUS. (*Sits by her.*) If anyone, anyone at all, knows I am here and not in the compound, you realize it is the end of everything as we know it.

CRANE. No, I hadn't realized that.

CYRUS. I am a prime candidate for kidnapping. Without me to make decisions, the conglomerate would crumble like a house of cards, there would be a panic on Wall Street, another Black Tuesday.

CRANE. Then perhaps you'd better go home.

CYRUS. (*Draws a contract from his pocket. It is several sheets, thick covered in blue paper, and folded in thirds.*) Not until I have your signature on this piece of paper.

CRANE. (*Rises and goes to windows.*) I appreciate your coming out of hiding to see me and I am flattered by your offer, but I must insist you contact my agent.

CYRUS. You sign here and I'll buy your agent. (*Another CRASH from the kitchen. He crosses to her in a panic.*) They're after me.

CRANE. Who?

CYRUS. Terrorists. (*Goes above sofa.*) They're everywhere.

CRANE. (*Goes to him.*) Then go. This is a very complicated evening, believe me.

CYRUS. I don't leave here without your signature. (*Opens closet and goes in.*) Think it over. (*Closes door.*)

CRANE. (*Wearily.*) Why do they always go in the closet?

CYRUS. (*Pokes his head out.*) Knock three times when you're ready to sign. (*Closes door.*)

CRANE. (*Takes tray of coffee to kitchen door calling.*) Are you all right, Jewel?

JEWEL. (*Opens kitchen door.*) I'm perfect. Can't say the same for the dishes.

CRANE. Forget it. We left a damage deposit. (JEWEL *takes tray and goes back into kitchen.* CRANE *is pouring another drink as* KATE *comes downstairs.*)

KATE. Joel is resting comfortably. Things have calmed down.

CRANE. You don't know. You just don't know.

KATE. You found the microdot?

CRANE. I haven't had time. Jewel is wrecking the kitchen and I have a surprise for you in the closet.

KATE. (*Looking at drink.*) How many of those have you had?

CRANE. Not enough.

KATE. And there is something in the closet?

CRANE. Um-hmm.

KATE. Do I get three guesses?

CRANE. I'll give you a dollar if you get it.

KATE. Cyrus D. Conway.

CRANE. (*Amazed.*) What?

KATE. Cyrus D. Conway.

CRANE. Write yourself a check for one dollar.

KATE. You're saying Cyrus D. Conway is standing in that closet?

CRANE. How did you ever guess him?

KATE. Because he is a recluse and never goes anywhere.

CRANE. Unless he wants something.

KATE. (*Goes to closet.*) You're kidding? He's not in there.

CRANE. You say he isn't. I say he is. Double or nothing?

KATE. You're on.

CRANE. Watch this. (*Knocks three times on desk.*)

CYRUS. (*Opens door with contract in hand.*) Ready to sign?

CRANE. No, but I'm thinking.

CYRUS. I'll wait. (*Closes door, has not seen* KATE *who stands to the* R.)

KATE. That was really Cyrus D. Conway?

CRANE. In the expensive flesh.

KATE. I won't have to write that check.

CRANE. Goody.

KATE. Do you mind if I look again?

CRANE. Be my guest. (KATE *opens the door.* CYRUS *is standing there.*)

CYRUS. If you're a terrorist, my company will pay nothing for me. Absolutely nothing.

KATE. I'm Kate Bixley, Mrs. Hammond's secretary.

CRANE. My flying fingers.

CYRUS. How do you do. I'm John Smith.

KATE. I know who you are. Mr. Conway.

CYRUS. Shh! Keep it secret. Terrorists, you know. Persuade Mrs. Hammond to sign with me. I'll give you a percent of the action. (*Closes door.*)

KATE. Sign what?

CRANE. He wants the rights to my next book.

KATE. Tell him to contact your agent.

CRANE. He's very adamant. (*Goes Up* C., *points as he did.*) He pointed at me and said, "I want you."

KATE. Sounds like Uncle Sam.

CRANE. I already said that.

KATE. You don't suppose—

CRANE. (*Moves above desk.*) I suppose nothing this entire evening.

KATE. —he has come for the microdot?

CRANE. (*Puts glass down on bar.*) That's it. He's not really Conway at all.

KATE. Recluses are eccentric and that one is definitely eccentric.

CRANE. Do we know what Conway is supposed to look like?

KATE. (*Crosses to her.*) I've seen pictures of him when he was a lot younger. It could be he.

CRANE. Let's ask him a question no one else would know.

KATE. Perfect. We'll trap him. How do I get him out?

CRANE. Knock three times.

KATE. It's like a seance. Suppose we get Kubla Khan? (*Knocks three times.*)

CYRUS. (*Opens door.*) Ready to sign?

KATE. (*Goes to him.*) We're not sure you are who you say you are.

CYRUS. How clever of you. You're my kind of people. You're going to ask me a question, aren't you?

KATE. Right. What is your grandmother's maiden name?

CYRUS. Krastopolous. (*Closes door.*)

KATE. (*To* CRANE.) There you are. Krastopolous.

EXIT WHO?

CRANE. (*Goes to* KATE.) Is that right?

KATE. How the hell do I know?

CRANE. Then why did you ask it?

KATE. I thought you'd know.

CRANE. (*Crosses above desk.*) That was a lousy idea. A master spy would always know the background of the person he's impersonating.

KATE. (*Moves above sofa.*) That's why you're the author and I'm the secretary. You're the clever one. (*There are THREE KNOCKS on the outside front door.*)

CYRUS. (*Closet door opens immediately.*) Ready?

KATE. That's not for you. (*Closes closet as* CRANE *goes to front door.*)

CRANE. With my luck that will be Jimmy Hoffa. (*Opens door and* WILFRED *is there.*)

WILFRED. (*Comes in.*) Sorry I'm late.

CRANE. You're not. You—

WILFRED. I seem to be the first one here anyway. (*Goes to bar as* CRANE *closes front door.*) Ah, an open bar. That's much simpler, I always think. Why spend your whole time mixing drinks. (*Pours drink.*) Of course if it's a really big affair like a wedding reception then it's advisable to be catered. I mean, hundreds of people, you just can't do it all yourself.

CRANE. No, I—

WILFRED. And all those little hors d'oeuvres and canapes to make. Catered is the only way. (*Sees cookies.*) Chocolate chip cookies. Clever of you. No hors d' oeuvres. Ah, delicious.

CRANE. Colonel, would you mind—

WILFRED. (*Has the pitcher in his hand.*) Getting some water? Not at all. (*Starts for kitchen.*) Glad to be back from the trenches. No time for cocktails there. Cannon to the left of us, Cannon to the right of us, But into the jaws of death rose the six hundred. (*Exits.*)

KATE. Maybe he'll ride right out through the kitchen.

CRANE. He's my odds on favorite for the master spy.

KATE. He does have the perfect cover for going anywhere at any time and no one questions him.

CRANE. But it isn't midnight and already we have (*Points to closet.*) that one in there who's suspicious and that one (*Points to kitchen.*) in there who's suspicious.

KATE. (*To upstairs.*) And what about up there?

CRANE. Joel?

KATE. He was the first one here and who has a more perfect cover for being here at midnight?

CRANE. And there are others.

KATE. Who?

CRANE. Think.

KATE. You mean—?

LYDIA. (*Comes in windows carrying tote bag.*) Here I am.

CRANE. The defense rests.

LYDIA. (*Goes below sofa to* CRANE.) I had trouble finding the third book. They'd filed it under "Romance" right next to Fannie Hurst.

CRANE. I don't think Fannie would have approved.

LYDIA. (*Goes to desk.*) There's no page 161 in her books and I've read them all. Here we are. (*Takes copies of* CRANE'S *books from her back and bangs them on the desk one at a time.*) One. Two.

CRANE. (*To* KATE *who is by closet door.*) Kate.

LYDIA. Three.

CYRUS. (*Opens door on third bang of book.*) Ready?

KATE. (*As she leans against closet door closing it.*) No.

LYDIA. (*Turns to* KATE.) Pardon me? Was that you?

KATE. (*Leaning nonchalantly against door.*) Yes. Frog in my throat. (*Clears her throat.*)

CRANE. Her voice slips sometimes. Before it changed she was a basso.

LYDIA. Isn't that backwards?

KATE. (*Moves to R. of sofa.*) Medical phenomena. In our high school production of SHOW-BOAT I even sang "Old Man River".

CRANE. And that was before ERA.

LYDIA. You girls are full of surprises. I can't wait to interview you. But, for tonight, all I need is your signature on these three for the library and this one for me. (*Pulls out a fourth book.*)

CRANE. My pleasure. (*Sits at desk to sign them.*)

WILFRED. (*Comes in from kitchen with water pitcher and goes Down C.*) I am bearing water like Gunga Din. I knew him, you know. "I'm a better man than you are, Gunga Din."

LYDIA. (*Crosses to him.*) That's backwards. It's "You're a better man than I am."

WILFRED. He may have been better than you but he was a damn sight worse than I am. (*Puts pitcher on bar.*)

CRANE. You two know each other, of course? (*Signs books.*)

LYDIA. Sometimes. Do you recognize me today, Colonel?

WILFRED. You're certainly not Gunga Din.

LYDIA. That's right.

WILFRED. You're Lydia Pinkham.

LYDIA. Oh, dear.

WILFRED. No, Scott. Lydia Pinkham was my first wife. (*Crosses to her.*) Glad you could come to the party. Will it be in the society column?

LYDIA. I didn't know there was a party.

CRANE. There isn't.

WILFRED. Then what is Julia Child doing in your kitchen?

LYDIA. (*Going towards kitchen.*) Julia Child here? You must know everyone, Mrs. Hammond—

CRANE. It's Jewel. She's cleaning up from dinner.

LYDIA. I should have known better.

WILFRED. (*Goes above chair* C.) Isn't Julia Child, eh? And there's no party? Perhaps I'm in the wrong place again. I'll just call Mabel from this phone booth. (*Whips into the closet and closes the door.*)

KATE. Colonel, wait.

LYDIA. (*Goes Up* C.) He does have a certain elfin charm, doesn't he?

CRANE. I think he's found Never-Never Land.

LYDIA. Mrs. Hammond, quickly, before we're disturbed again. I know what's happening here and what's going to happen.

CRANE. You're him—her—midnight and all that?

LYDIA. Let me explain, I—

WILFRED. (*Comes out of closet.*) Light's out in the phone booth. Have to report that to the phone company. What do we pay bills for? Need another phone, too. There was someone ahead of me.

KATE. You can use that phone, Colonel. (*Indicates the phone on desk.*)

WILFRED. Damned impolite fellow in there. Took the dime right out of my hand.

LYDIA. You think there is someone else in there?

WILFRED. (*Goes to her.*) Reminds me of that dark garage where I used to meet that fellow right before Watergate.

LYDIA. Colonel, there is no one in there.

WILFRED. Oh, yes, there is.

LYDIA. (*To* KATE *as she goes to closet.*) We have to prove these things to him once in awhile.

KATE. Let's just ignore it.

LYDIA. I'll show you, Colonel. (*Opens closet door to show* COLONEL. *She is standing to the* R. *of it so she can't see in but the others can.* CYRUS *is standing there.*) There. (*Closes the door.*) Now we know the truth, don't we?

WILFRED. (*Pleased he was right.*) We certainly do.

CRANE. I'm glad that's settled. (*Hands books to* LYDIA.) Here you are, Lydia. All signed.

LYDIA. (*Crosses to desk.*) Thank you so much.

WILFRED. (*To* KATE.) I had to sign books once at Doubledays. You may not know it but I wrote WAR AND PEACE.

KATE. Do you know Russian?

WILFRED. The English version was called GONE WITH THE WIND.

KATE. (*Sits Down* R.) Frankly, Colonel, I don't give a damn.

CRANE. A drink, Lydia?

LYDIA. Heavens, no. (*Puts books in tote bag.*) I'll have enough at the Morgan's. They're having a few people over this evening.

WILFRED. Morgan's? That's where I'm supposed to be. This isn't it?

LYDIA. No, Colonel. Come along, I'll take you with me.

WILFRED. Splendid. Always delighted to escort a beautiful woman.

LYDIA. (*To* CRANE.) And I'll be back later to finish that conversation we started.

CRANE. Maybe tomorrow.

LYDIA. Later is better. Colonel, my arm. (WILFRED

takes it as she leads him above sofa to windows.) And when we get there, if you'll be kind enough to make me a Scotch and soda.

WILFRED. They're have liquor?

LYDIA. I certainly hope so.

WILFRED. Wonder where they got it. It's a devilish thing, this prohibition. (THEY *are out.*)

CRANE. (*Crosses Down* C.) Did you hear her, Kate? She wants to come back later.

KATE. (*Crosses in to sofa.*) She's the spy.

CRANE. If she is, they have a personnel shortage over there.

KATE. Remember what Joel said. "It could be anyone."

CRANE. (*Sits on sofa.*) I still lean towards the Colonel.

KATE. How about Vernon? He's too Pa Kettle to be legitimate.

CRANE. And don't forget Jewel in the kitchen.

KATE. (*Goes above sofa.*) And the recluse who's closeted.

CRANE. If we only had a computer. We need someone to analyze all this.

KATE. Maybe Joel's coming back to the present. I'll check and see. (*Goes to stairs.*)

CRANE. (*Goes Up* C.) And I'll try to get rid of Cyrus D. Conway.

KATE. Before they confront each other.

CRANE. Like Stanley and Livingston.

KATE. The Colonel was there, you know. Stanley really said, "Mr. Livingston *and* Colonel Wooster, I presume." (*Exits upstairs.*)

CRANE. (*Knocks three times on desk slowly. The closet doesn't open. She goes to the closet door and knocks again.*) Olly—olly—oxen free! (*Opens the door and closet is empty.*) Mr. Conway. Cyrus. (*Goes through closet into library. Off Stage.*) It's me. Mrs. Hammond, your favorite author. (*Comes out Up c. as* KATE *rushes downstairs.*)

CRANE AND KATE. He's gone!

CRANE. Joel, too?

KATE. And the recluse?

CRANE. The library window is open.

KATE. There's a convenient drainpipe outside the guest room window.

JEWEL. (*Marches in from kitchen to between the two of them.*) I'm finished. Have to hurry. Late for Bingo. I'm three games behind already. Don't go clumping through the kitchen. My dough is rising.

CRANE. You're baking?

JEWEL. Don't like store bought, do you?

CRANE. No.

JEWEL. (*Turns on* KATE.) Do you?

KATE. Heaven forfend.

JEWEL. I'll be back after Bingo, after it's risen.

KATE. Is it Easter?

CRANE. Kate, that's sacrilegious.

JEWEL. (*Opens door.*) If you bed down early, I'll be quiet.

CRANE. Can't I do the bread for you?

JEWEL. No one touches my bread, I'm off, I must have missed four games by now. I'm best on the diagonal. (*Exits and* CRANE *closes the door.*)

KATE. She must be a whiz on Little Round Robin.

CRANE. So she's coming back later, too.

KATE. So is everyone else in town.

CRANE. (*Sits on* L. *side of sofa.*) I am going to sit a minute and think.

KATE. Let's put our feet up. (*Sits on sofa and they both put their feet up facing each other.*)

CRANE. A few moments of quiet meditation never hurts. (THEY *close their eyes.*)

KATE. When I close me eyes, I don't see spots. I see microdots.

CRANE. Anyway, it's quiet.

KATE. Yes, too quiet.

JEWEL. (*Comes bounding in front door waving a folded piece of paper in front of her.*) Guess what?

CRANE. You're not good on the diagonal.

JEWEL. This was on the windshield of your car. (*Hands* CRANE *the paper.*) If it's a ticket I can get it fixed for you. Verne owes me a favor from the time I saved him from drownin'.

CRANE. Jewel, how heroic.

JEWEL. He was floatin' downstream during the Spring thaw.

CRANE. You threw him a life preserver?

JEWEL. Nope. An oak tree. (*Goes to door.*) Well, I'm missin' Bingo. Be up to intermission now and I can get me a Diet Pepsi.

KATE. That's a wise girl.

JEWEL. And half a dozen jelly donuts. (*Exits, closing front door.*)

KATE. It couldn't be a ticket.

CRANE. It isn't. Listen. (*Reads the note.*) "You better have the plans or else."

KATE. Or else what?

CRANE. "Please turn over." (*Turns paper to other side.*) "Or else you know what."

KATE. Is it signed?

CRANE. No. Anyway, whoever it is saved a stamp.

KATE. (*Rises and goes to windows.*) But we don't have the plans and I don't want his "or else".

CRANE. (*Rises.*) Maybe this is from the double agent with the twenty thousand. The master spy may know we don't have the plans.

KATE. If he thinks we don't have them then he won't show up.

CRANE. But he must so we can turn him over to Joel.

KATE. How can we be sure he'll come here?

CRANE. I know. (*Goes to phone.*)

KATE. What are you going to do? Remember the life you save may be yours—and mine.

CRANE. (*Into phone.*) Mabel, is Western Union still open? . . . You are? (*To* KATE.) She's Western Union, too. (*Into phone.*) I want to send a telegram. It goes to General Lester Burroughs.

KATE. Who's that?

CRANE. (*To* KATE.) I'm making it up. (*Into phone.*) The Pentagon. Washington, D.C. Here's the message. Dear Lester. Have the plans. Leaving with them tomorrow morning. Sign it Crane.

KATE. Oh, this isn't wise.

CRANE. (*Into phone.*) Thank you, Mabel. (*Hangs up.*)

KATE. What happens when that's delivered?

CRANE. It can't be since there isn't any General Burroughs, but Mabel will tell everyone we have some plans so the master spy is bound to find out. (*Goes to* KATE.) Kate, how much liquor do we have over there?

KATE. Why?

CRANE. Because we're giving a midnight party.

KATE. But who's coming?

CRANE. Everyone, Kate. Everyone.

CURTAIN

EXIT WHO?

Scene 2.

(*The same evening. Shortly before midnight.* KATE *is staring out the windows.* CRANE *is sitting on the sofa doing a crossword puzzle from the paper.*)

CRANE. What are you staring at?
KATE. Nothing. There's so much of it. Back in the city, I can at least look in the apartments across the way and watch the robberies.
CRANE. (*Writes word in puzzle.*) Oh, there's one I know.
KATE. How can you sit there doing a crossword puzzle when it's almost midnight?
CRANE. It's relaxing.
KATE. (*Looks at closet.*) I wonder . . . (*Goes to it and quickly opens it.*) I don't know what I would have done if someone had been in there.
CRANE. (*At puzzle.*) Oh, no!
KATE. (*Goes above sofa.*) Have you thought of something?
CRANE. It doesn't fit.
KATE. What?
CRANE. (*Showing her puzzle.*) Look. A best-selling suspense author in seven letters.
KATE. Fleming. What did you put?
CRANE. Hammond. (*Crosses to bar and puts paper down.*) Let's have a drink.
KATE. I'm too nervous.
CRANE. (*Holds up plate.*) Cookie?
KATE. (*Pacing to windows.*) They're not cookies. They're doorstops.
CRANE. I've never seen you so nervous. It's not midnight yet.

KATE. (*Turns to her.*) And what happens when it is? Do you honestly think someone is going to sneak up behind you at the witching hour and say—

VERNON. (*Appears behind* KATE.) Hello, Ladies. (*Tips his hat.* KATE *gives a surprised gasp and turns.*)

KATE. Vernon, you scared the pants right off me.

VERNON. (*Smiles.*) Ayah.

CRANE. She doesn't mean literally, Verne.

VERNON. Ayah. Can see she don't.

CRANE. (*Crosses below chair* C.) What can we do for you?

VERNON. (*Goes below sofa.*) It's what I can do for you. I been prowlin' around out there, hidin' in the shadows as it were, and it seems I had company.

KATE. Who?

VERNON. Don't know that.

CRANE. What were you doing out there in the first place?

VERNON. (*Crosses* C.) Protectin' you ladies.

KATE. (*Crosses below sofa.*) From what?

VERNON. From midnight.

CRANE. You know.

VERNON. Whole town knows. Mabel's got loose lips.

CRANE. So you've come to watch over us?

VERNON. I've come for the military installations. (*Pulls out revolver.*)

KATE. It's you!

CRANE. Vernon Cookley!

VERNON. Ain't sportin' comin' before midnight but then all's fair in love and war.

CRANE. And which is this?

VERNON. Don't confuse me. Just give me the plans.

CRANE. But we don't have them.

VERNON. Yes, you do.

CRANE. No, we don't.
VERNON. Yes, you do.
KATE. No, we don't.
VERNON. Yes, you do.
CRANE. (*Goes to desk and puts drink down.*) This could go on all night. We do not have the plans. We know they're supposed to be here, but we don't know where.
VERNON. You're sure?
CRANE. You can search me if you want.
VERNON. Ayah.
KATE. Don't you touch her, you old lecher.
VERNON. Supposed to have one of them prison matrons search the ladies. I'll take your word for it, Mrs. Hammond.
CRANE. Thank you. Vernon.
VERNON. (*Puts gun away.*) Don't need this no more.
KATE. Is that all? You're not going to shoot us?
VERNON. What for?
KATE. (*Crosses to him dramatically.*) We don't have the plans. We're expendable. Cover your tracks. Get rid of us. We can prove who you are. Don't be a fool. Kill us.
CRANE. Kate, think what you're saying.
KATE. (*Realizes.*) I didn't mean it, Verne. (*Moves away below sofa.*) God knows, I didn't mean it.
VERNON. Didn't think you did. (*To* CRANE.) Hysterical type, ain't she?
CRANE. A trifle overwrought. Vernon, what are you going to do now that we don't have the plans?
VERNON. Wait till midnight and catch whoever comes for them.
KATE. You're not he — him — it?
CRANE. (*Sits chair* C.) I knew you weren't the spy.
VERNON. So a spy wants 'em, eh? Figured as much

when I heard they was military installations. Good thing for you I'm with the government.

CRANE. The FBI?

KATE. The CIA?

VERNON. None of them lettered places. I'm the Sheriff so I'm part of the judicial system of this here country. I catch the spy, it will be a feather in my cap. 'Cept I don't own a cap. Have a fur-lined huntin' hat though. With flaps. Comes down over the ears like this. (*Demonstrates.*)

CRANE. I'm so glad you're on our side.

KATE. (*Sits on sofa.*) I'm not so sure.

VERNON. Thought maybe I could get the plans before midnight. It's past my bedtime.

CRANE. (*Crosses to bar.*) Verne, you deserve a drink.

VERNON. Ayah.

CRANE. (*Pours Scotch.*) You see, we're looking for the plans, too. We don't know who's coming to get them and we thought it might be you.

VERNON. (*Sits chair C.*) Nope. T'ain't me.

KATE. Or Colonel Wooster or Lydia Scott or Jewel or—well, there have been several other strange people around today. (CRANE *goes to* VERNON *with drink.*)

VERNON. Might be any of 'em. (*Swallows drink.*) Thanks.

KATE. You're quite a drinker, Verne.

VERNON. This is nothing' compared to what the wife does with dandelion wine. First year ain't much, but the second year it would raise a moustache on a speckled trout. Mind if I have a cookie?

CRANE. (*Passes plate.*) Help yourself.

KATE. You have good teeth?

VERNON. Montgomery-Ward gave me a six month guarantee. (*Eats cookie.*)

CRANE. Verne, it's almost midnight. If the spy knows

you're here I don't think he'll make a try for the plans.

VERNON. Ayah, might be turned off by the sight of a savage law officer.

CRANE. Why don't you go back outside and wait till we see who shows up?

VERNON. (*Rises.*) You write them books so you must be right.

CRANE. Don't go too far away. We may need help.

VERNON. (*Sotto voce.*) I'll just go over to the windows there and pretend I'm saying good night real subtle like, and then I'll slip off among the shadows.

CRANE. Perfect.

VERNON. (*Crosses to windows. Sotto voce.*) Don't be too scared if I pull my gun. Don't have no bullets in it.

KATE. Why not?

VERNON. Never used bullets since my brother-in-law got his finger shot off. Minister got real mad at him.

CRANE. The minister?

VERNON. Brother-in-law was the accompanist for the choir. Now he has to leave out all the notes he used to play with this finger. (*Holds up finger.*)

CRANE. The soloist must be furious.

VERNON. Can't be. She shot him. Well, here goes my act. (*Projects very loud acting to the hilt.*) Good night, Mrs. Hammond.

CRANE. So nice of you to drop by.

VERNON. Good night, Miss Bixley.

KATE. Good night, Vernon. (*Sotto voce.*) You're doing very well.

VERNON. (*Sotto voce.*) Thank you. (*Loud.*) See you tomorrow morning.

CRANE. Good night.

VERNON. What about ten o'clock? Not before then. Won't see you before then. (*Starts off and comes back.*)

I have to wash the windows in the Court House. (*Sotto voce.*) I don't really. They call that an ad-lib.

CRANE. Very clever of you.

VERNON. (*Sotto voce.*) Now I'll make like a shadow and disappear. (*Draws himself up as thin as possible and slips out of sight.*)

CRANE. (*Crosses in Down C.*) At least we know the master spy isn't Verne.

KATE. Unless he was being brilliant to find out if we had the plans. How much time do we have?

CRANE. A little over five minutes.

KATE. (*Rises.*) I will have that drink.

CRANE. (*To bar and mixes Scotch and water.*) Good for you.

KATE. I wish I would have changed my will before I left the city.

CRANE. Don't be gloomy.

KATE. I left my good Balenciaga suit to my cousin and she's gained so much weight she'll have to use it as a throw rug.

CRANE. (*Hands drink across desk to* KATE.) I'm going to phone Richard. I just want to hear his voice.

KATE. (*Sits chair C.*) The only voice I want to hear is one of those New York derelicts saying, "Any extra change?" How can there be such a thing as extra change?

CRANE. (*Going through desk drawers and piling papers on top.*) Do you suppose there's a phone book here.

KATE. It wouldn't be Los Angeles anyway. Get information. Go ahead. Give Mabel a thrill. Her last long distance call was probably to down the road apiece.

CRANE. (*Starts putting papers back in drawers when she notices some store coupons and a shopping list held together with a paper clip.*) Look, here's some coupons.

KATE. I'll take them in case I ever see a store again. (*Gets them and sits in desk chair.*)

CRANE. (*Holding phone at above desk.*) Where is Mabel?

KATE. She must go to the john sometime. (*Going through coupons.*) These are no good. They're all for frozen dinners; Lasagna, Turkey, Macaroni. The only way they taste good is if you lick them like a popsicle.

CRANE. (*Into phone.*) Hello . . . hello . . . (*To* KATE.) It is dead. No one's there. (*Hangs up.*)

KATE. They've cut the wires. You should have known that. You always have that happen.

CRANE. I should have paid more attention to myself. (*Puts rest of papers in desk drawers. Looks at coupons.*) I almost feel sorry for him. Spying is such a lonely life.

KATE. If only we knew where that damned microdot was.

CRANE. Oh. I know that.

KATE. You don't.

CRANE. I do.

KATE. You do?

CRANE. It is almost midnight, we don't have time for this idle banter.

KATE. But where is the microdot?

CRANE. (*Goes Down* C.) Now I know why you're the secretary and I'm the author. (*Looks at watch.*) Less than one minute till midnight.

KATE. Where shall we stand?

CRANE. Right here in the middle of the room. We'll meet the spy standing up.

KATE. (*Goes to her.*) Maybe I'd better hold on. (*They stand clutching each other.*) How much longer?

EXIT WHO?

CRANE. Twenty seconds.
KATE. What if his watch is slow?
CRANE. Fifteen.
KATE. What if your watch is slow?
CRANE. Ten.
KATE. What if he's had a flat tire?
CRANE. Five — four — three — two — one — midnight! (*A pause.*)
KATE. Is it midnight before the clock strikes twelve or after?
CRANE. If it's after, midnight is right now!
LYDIA. (*Comes in windows.*) I'm back.
JOEL. (*In from closet.*) I still can't remember anything.
WILFRED. (*In front door.*) Is this the right house?
JEWEL. (*In from the kitchen.*) My bread rose. (*As each person comes in,* CRANE *and* KATE *turns toward them.*)
CRANE. What are you all doing here? (*They all start to talk at once.* CRANE *tops them as she goes Up* C.) Quiet! Quiet! Quiet! (*They fall silent.*)
KATE. (*Sinks on sofa.*) This hasn't accomplished a thing.
CRANE. Out! I want everyone to get out and leave us alone. Tomorrow. You can call tomorrow. (*Goes to* LYDIA.) Lydia, I'll give you an interview in the morning. (*To* JOEL.) Will you please leave with her?
JOEL. Do I know her?
LYDIA. (*As she leaves by windows.*) I can walk myself home thank you. (JOEL *follows her out.*)
CRANE. Mr. Conway, see me in the morning with pen in hand.
CYRUS. I hope no one here recognizes me. (*Exits.*)
WILFRED. Don't tell me. I'm in the wrong house

again. (*Exits front door.*)

CRANE. (*To* JEWEL.) Jewel, please put the dough in the freezer until morning.

JEWEL. But you need a home-cooked breakfast.

CRANE. (*As pushes her out the kitchen door.*) If you do as I ask, I'll let you make us some red flannel hash.

JEWEL. It's a deal. (*Exits.*)

CRANE. There. That's done.

KATE. But, Crane, who is it? They all showed up.

CRANE. Yes, but the master spy will be back. He knows the microdot is here and he assumes we coudln't say anything with everyone else here.

KATE. So what do we do?

CRANE. (*Goes* C.) Put out the lights like we're going to bed.

KATE. (*Rises.*) You think I'm staying here with the lights out?

CRANE. You can go upstairs alone.

KATE. I'm staying here.

CRANE. Where should we hide? (*Puts LIGHTS out by Up* C. *switch. Only DESK LIGHT remains on.*)

KATE. I'd suggest the closet but it's always full.

CRANE. In plain sight, that's always best. Duck down in front of the sofa. (KATE *does and* CRANE *puts out DESK LIGHT. Only a MOONLIGHT WASH fills the stage.*)

KATE. I haven't played hide and seek since I was eight.

CRANE. (*Gets down beside her.*) Did they find you?

KATE. Always.

CRANE. Shh. I hear someone. (JEWEL *comes in from kitchen. The following scene is all sotto voce.* JEWEL *goes to desk.*)

KATE. It's Jewel.

CRANE. Someone else is coming.

JEWEL. (*Hears noise outside windows.*) Dadgumit! (*Starts back for kitchen but the door slowly swings open towards her, pinning her against the* L. *wall.* JOEL *comes in and as the door swings back* JEWEL *goes with it into the kitchen.*)

JOEL. Mrs. Hammond. Miss Bixley. (*Walks Up* C.) Where are you? (*Hears noise outside windows and goes into the closet.*)

KATE. That was Joel. Is he the spy?

CRANE. Here comes another. (LYDIA *comes in windows and starts for desk.*)

KATE. Lydia Scott. I knew it. (LYDIA *rummages through desk drawers.*)

CRANE. Don't be too sure.

LYDIA. I'll win a Pulitzer for this. (*Hears a loud "Psst!" from windows. Runs Up* C., *decides on the stairs and goes up them.*)

KATE. (*After another "Psst!" from windows.*) Either someone else is coming or you have a flat tire.

CRANE. Time for Mr. Conway.

CYRUS. (*Comes in windows.*) Mrs. Hammond. Thank you for not giving me away. Now we can sign the contract. (*Goes Up* C.) Mrs. Hammond. (*Front door starts to open slowly and he goes into the library.*)

WILFRED. (*Comes in front door.*) I could have sworn I left the lights on. (*Goes to desk after putting on LIGHTS Up* C.) It's not like me to be forgetful. (*DESK LIGHT on. Starts down, sees the girls hiding.*) Oh, hello.

CRANE. Good evening, Colonel.

WILFRED. You dropped something? Can I help you look for it?

KATE. (*As they get up.*) Why did you have to put the lights on?

WILFRED. I always do when it's dark. (*Moves away* L.) Except when I was blind, of course. Four months in the hospital after the accident. I remember the morning they removed the bandages. The first thing I saw was the doctor. It was the woman who had run me over and I never knew it.

CRANE. That was THE MAGNIFICENT OBSESSION with Irene Dunne.

KATE. The remake was with Jane Wyman.

WILFRED. I never go to the movies. Did you find the guest rooms all right?

CRANE. Colonel Wooster, this is not your house.

WILFRED. I've done it again, eh?

KATE. On purpose?

VERNON. (*Comes in windows with gun drawn.*) Reach!

CRANE. Verne, thank you for coming so quickly.

VERNON. It's the Colonel. He's the one who showed up.

CRANE. So did everyone else. If you call them in, I think I have the answers for you.

VERNON. If you say so.

KATE. Crane, are you sure?

CRANE. Mostly.

VERNON. (*Calls out windows.*) Everyone is here in the name of the law.

CRANE. They're not outside, Verne. They're all in here.

VERNON. (*Comes back in.*) Everyone in here in the name of the law! (LYDIA *comes downstairs,* JEWEL *from kitchen,* JOEL *from closet.*)

CRANE. Come along, we know you're all here, and we know what you're after. (*She crosses Up* C., KATE *to above sofa,* WILFRED *to* L. *of desk.*)

LYDIA. (*Above desk.*) I only came back to tell you I have a direct line to The Times if anything important happens.

JEWEL. I'm puttin' the dough in the freezer.

VERNON. How much you got out there, twenty thousand?

CRANE. No, Verne, bread dough.

VERNON. I was quick on the uptake, wasn't I?

KATE. (*Looking around.*) Mr. Conway isn't here.

CRANE. (*Calls.*) Cyrus, I'll sign your contract. (*Closet opens immediately and hits* JOEL *who falls to the floor.*)

CYRUS. Got it right here. (*Looks down at* JOEL.) I hope he's your agent.

KATE. Is he dead?

CRANE. (*As the three help him to stand.*) With any luck, this is just what the doctor ordered.

VERNON. You mean one of them chiropractors?

CRANE. He's just dazed.

LYDIA. If it's not murder it won't make the front page.

CRANE. (*To* JOEL.) Who are you?

JOEL. You know who I am, Mrs. Hammond. I'm Joel Dover.

CRANE. Do you remember everything?

JOEL. I recall going to the kitchen and then the door opened and she—(*Points to* KATE.)

KATE. It was an accident.

JEWEL. Shouldn't have been in my kitchen.

CRANE. Do you remember what's happened in between?

JOEL. Not quite. Who are all these people?

WILFRED. They're all guests. I am giving a houseparty.

CRANE. It's all right, Mr. Dover. I know where the plans are. (*Ad-lib from all which is topped by* JOEL.)

JOEL. They are government property!

CRANE. Very simple. They're pasted inside this issue of the New York Times. (*Takes from the desk.*) Anyone can have them who wants them. (CYRUS, LYDIA, JEWEL, *and* WILFRED *reach for them.* VERNON *pulls his gun and yells.*)

VERNON. Hold it right there or I'll shoot. (*They all stop in their tracks.*)

JOEL. But who is the master spy?

CRANE. Obviously, none of these people.

KATE. But it must be one of them.

CRANE. It isn't because they all rushed for the plans, didn't they?

KATE. The real spy wouldn't have because he is the only one, besides us, who knows the plans are in a microdot.

JEWEL. What's a microdot?

CYRUS. I thought I was getting the contract signed.

LYDIA. If those had been the plans I would have gotten a by-line in Newsweek.

CRANE. All right, everyone get comfortable and I'll explain everything. (*During the following,* LYDIA *sits in chair* C., VERNON *stays by the windows,* JEWEL *sits in the desk chair,* JOEL *perches on the back of the sofa,* CYRUS *sits on the sofa,* WILFRED *wanders into the library.*)

JEWEL. (*To* VERNON.) Put the gun away, Verne. We all know it isn't loaded.

JOEL. If you get those plans, I'll see you're nominated for a Congressional Medal of Honor.

CYRUS. And I'll give you another ten percent of the gross.

LYDIA. An exclusive, that's all I want.

CRANE. What none of you know, except Joel, is that the military installations are on a microdot no bigger than the end of a pencil. The man who lived here last month left it to be picked up tonight at midnight but the master spy, someone right here in the village, didn't know where it was. Well, I know. This told me. (*Picks up the shopping list.*)

KATE. That shopping list?

CRANE. It has everything for the poor man to cook himself dinner: frozen soup, hearty beef pies, Sara Lee cheesecake.

JOEL. What's so unusual about that? That's the way I cook.

JEWEL. You poor man.

CRANE. But there is also flour and baking powder on the list.

KATE. Maybe he was going to make papier maché ornaments for his Christmas tree.

CRANE. There is no indication he cooked anything in that kitchen but frozen food. Then why the flour and baking powder? To hide the microdot in the one thing he did cook.

KATE. Those! (*Points to the plate which has one cookie left.*)

CRANE. (*Holds up plate with one cookie.*) Right. These chocolate chip cookies.

KATE. Then someone ate the microdot.

CRANE. No, if anyone had, he would have choked. No one did and there is one cookie left so here are the plans. (*Holds up cookie.*)

KATE. Incredible.

CRANE. Elementary, my dear Kate.

JOEL. (*Rises and moves by windows.*) But who is the spy?

CRANE. Who keeps track of everything that goes on in

the village? Who knows everyone's whereabouts? (*Holds up phone.*) Who is not at her post now?

ALL. Mabel! (*Closet door opens and* MABEL *is standing there with a gun. She is a typical looking, cheerful soul under ordinary circumstances but now she is hard and determined. She is dressed in a cotton dress.*)

MABEL. That's right, your trusty Mabel. (*Comes in and closes door.*) I could write enough about this village to make DALLAS look like a suburb. All these years, any time I wanted to find out anything I'd just listen in. Everyone trusted Mabel but Mabel trusted no one. Now I'm going back home with those plans and I'll be set for life. An apartment in the Kremlin. (*To* CRANE.) I would have given you twenty thousand dollars for that cookie but now it's mine for free.

CRANE. You made that phone call?

MABEL. Just in case you stumbled on the microdot and decided to skip town, I thought I'd buy you off. Nothing can stop me now. Hand over that cookie. (CRANE *passes the plate and* MABEL *takes the cookie.*) Just think, one lousy little cookie holds the answer to domination of the world's power. And it's mine now. All mine. (*Closet door opens hitting* MABEL, *cookie flies into* KATE'S *hands, and* CRANE *grabs the gun.*)

CRANE. Hold it right there.

KATE. I got the cookie. (*Crosses to table* R. *of sofa and starts crumbling cookie.*)

WILFRED. (*Comes out of closet holding Monopoly board.*) I thought we might like a game of Monopoly. I lived on Park Place once, you know. I remember —

JOEL. I'll take that gun, Mrs. Hammond.

CRANE. You can have it. I've never fired one. (*Hands him the gun.*)

WILFRED. No one wants to play? (*Returns to closet and closes door.*)

LYDIA. Mabel, I am shocked.

CYRUS. (*Crosses to the R. of the sofa.*) Perhaps we could discuss publishing your biography.

JEWEL. Does this mean Mabel isn't really Mabel? Who are you, Mabel?

MABEL. The real name's Petrushka. After World War II, I crossed the border from Canada. It was easy to get a job down here. You believed everything I told you about my past. So what finally happens? I'm caught by a second-rate author.

CRANE. Second-rate? I'll have you know that my books—

KATE. Help! These dots are all chocolate. No microdot.

MABEL. That's a laugh. Someone did eat it.

CRANE. Verne—(*Puts her hand out.*)

VERNON. Ayah.

CRANE. Let's have the other cookie.

VERNON. Ayah.

CRANE. I saw you snitch it earlier.

VERNON. I thought they was right tasty.

CRANE. (*Takes cookie and crumbles it on table R. of chair.*) It had better be here.

KATE. That's the way the cookie crumbles.

LYDIA. I'm getting my story after all.

CYRUS. (*Goes above sofa.*) You're too late. My conglomorate will have it into the papers by morning, onto GOOD MORNING, AMERICA on Monday, and into book form by Wednesday.

CRANE. Voila! Here is the microdot. (*Goes below sofa and shows it to* KATE.) It's ours!

LYDIA. (*Crosses to* CYRUS *at closet.*) Can't I call the Times? It's my first exclusive.

CYRUS. This story is mine. The meek shall not inherit the earth. (*Closet door opens and knocks him out.*)

WILFRED. (*Stands there with a Scrabble Board.*) Perhaps you'd rather play Scrabble.

CURTAIN

PROPERTY LIST

ACT ONE

On Stage:
Sheets covering chair Center and sofa
Vase on what-not shelf
Pile of books on desk
Phone with no dial on desk
Bottles, including Scotch, glasses, empty pitcher, etc. on bar
Clutter of papers in desk drawers

Off Right (French Windows):
Bunch of small flowers (Wilfred)

Off Up Left (Outside):
2 suitcases (Crane)
Purse (Crane)
Tall flowers in florist's paper (Crane)
Suitcase, portable typewriter (Kate)
Brief-case with blank paper, checkbook, pen (Kate)
Purse with pad and pencil (Lydia)
Large bag with groceries (Jewel)

Off Down Left (Kitchen):
Cubes of ice wrapped in kitchen towel (Kate)

ACT TWO

Scene 1.

On Stage:
Coffee service with pot

3 cups and saucers
Spoons on desk
Ice bucket with ice
Water pitcher partly filled on bar

Off Right (French Windows):
Blue covered folded contract (Cyrus)
Tote bag with 4 copies of CRANE's books (Lydia)

Off Up Left (Outside):
Folded note (Jewel)

Off Down Left (Kitchen):
Plate of eight chocolate chip cookies (Jewel)
Crash box for broken china (Jewel)
Water to fill on stage pitcher (Wilfred)

SCENE 2.

On stage:
N.Y. Times opened to crossword puzzle
Pencil on sofa (Crane)
Several cents-off coupons and shopping list paper clipped together in desk drawer

Off Right (French Windows):
Revolver (Vernon)
Cookie for his pocket (Vernon)

Off Up Right (Library):
Revolver (Mabel)
Monopoly game (Wilfred)
Scrabble board (Wilfred)

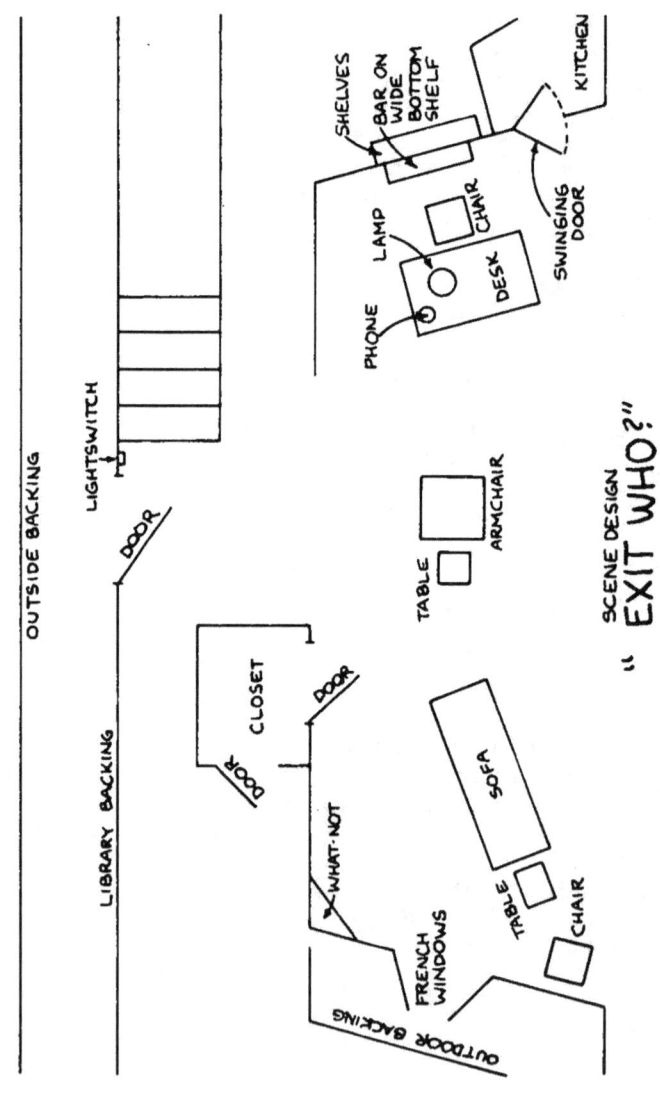

www.ingramcontent.com/pod-product-compliance
Lightning Source LLC
Chambersburg PA
CBHW072017290426
44109CB00018B/2263